BEHIND THE BLUE LINE

4/18

MY FIGHT AGAINST RACISM AND
DISCRIMINATION IN THE POLICE

BEHIND
THE
BLUE LINE

GURPAL VIRDI

Biteback Publishing

First published in Great Britain in 2018 by
Biteback Publishing Ltd
Westminster Tower
3 Albert Embankment
London SE1 7SP
Copyright © Gurpal Virdi 2018

ISBN 978-1-78590-321-2

10 9 8 7 6 5 4 3 2 1

A CIP catalogue record for this book is available from the British Library.

Set in Minion Pro

Printed and bound in Great Britain by
CPI Group (UK) Ltd, Croydon CR0 4YY

CONTENTS

To my family and friends who stood by me, and to those who put their heads above the parapet.

NOTE ON THE TEXT

All quotes have been transcribed verbatim from sources.

Any dialogue quoted from the trial proceedings is taken
from my notes, as well as from the official prosecution notes
relating to the trial. Anything that is not in quotations is my
own personal impression and also based on notes that
I made during the hearings.

The present laws of the United Kingdom impose a lifelong prohibition on disclosing the name of the complainant.
His name has therefore been changed in the following
account, along with the names of those associated with him,
and any background details that might identify him.

FOREWORD

SIR PETER BOTTOMLEY MP

When speaking about the police, what comes most to mind are stories of reliability, calm bravery and dedicated individuals.

I hold Gurpal Virdi in the highest regard, as both officer and friend, having known and admired him for nearly twenty years. It was an honour to be with his family at New Scotland Yard when senior officer Bernard Hogan-Howe apologised on behalf of the then Commissioner for the treatment Gurpal had been subjected to by the Metropolitan Police, and then awarded him the delayed special Commendation for exemplary conduct in the case of a near fatal attack on a foreign student.

How was it possible that such an impressive officer would be persecuted and prosecuted in both service and in retirement?

Stephen Lawrence lived and was murdered in my south-east London constituency. I was aware of many of the deficiencies in the police investigation of that attack. Gurpal set a higher standard for policing.

This book covers the consequences that followed Gurpal's commitment to combatting racism and to his initiatives following the west London case. He found the weapon, arrested two of the five suspects and visited the victim's home.

The troubles started when he asked whether it had been recorded as a potentially racially motivated attack.

Until cleared, Gurpal faced grim and persistent discriminatory action by his employer. I was one of those who stood by him and advocated his innocence.

I do not have the words to describe the horror I felt when the Crown Prosecution Service and the Metropolitan Police Service mismanaged the retirement case, sending it to trial.

It was heard in Southwark Crown Court and lasted over a week, ending with Gurpal's inevitable acquittal. In the public gallery, I watched and listened as prosecution witnesses, whose evidence was highly dubious or vague beyond belief, took to the stand.

It was clear that Gurpal was not guilty of misconduct in public office; he had not assaulted a youth in a police van. The accusations were absurd and unjustified.

There was no credible evidence that a crime had ever occurred and nothing indicating that Gurpal had even been present.

What has still not been adequately explained or justified is how, after fifteen months of professional investigation, the police could still brief the media that the 'victim' was under sixteen; how, despite all of the complainant's claimed statements of fact being contradicted by the prosecution's police witness or by the only official documents that the police had not destroyed, the charges were not dropped; how the investigators chose not to take a statement from the officer who had initially arrested the complainant; and, finally, how the police then failed to take a statement from Gurpal's accompanying officer, who, months later, witnessed Gurpal arresting this subsequent accuser without complaint for a traffic offence. Incompetence? Misplaced solidarity? Cock-up?

Before the trial, I wrote to police and prosecutors, outlining these concerns. Following Gurpal's acquittal, I made complaints to law officers, the Home Office, Sir Bernard Hogan-Howe, then the Commissioner of the Metropolitan Police, and to the Crown Prosecution Service with the Director of Public Prosecutions. I spoke directly to the Home Secretary, Theresa May.

Behind the Blue Line is the story of a good public servant. Without rancour, it details the obstacles, the prejudice and the official carelessness that can get in the way of a dedicated officer's career. We can learn from it. We must learn from it. These events should never be able to happen again.

The authorities must ask themselves the following question: why did they ever treat Gurpal in these ways over the decades? The best way forward would be for the government and the Met to conduct an official inquiry now.

Sir Peter Bottomley is a Conservative politician who has represented the West Worthing constituency since 1997.

● ● ●

DR RICHARD STONE

In my working life, I have seen too many stories of the injustices suffered by brave people who stick their head above the parapet and challenge racial inequality and injustice. This book by Gurpal Virdi is a first-class example of such a story. In it he describes, in a way that I have never before seen in print, a catalogue of victimisation and of totally unprofessional actions by the Metropolitan Police, putting their 'adversary' into positions of danger and of humiliation. It is essential that such stories are told. In the twenty years since 1999 there have been too many Virdi-type cases.

One day in 2000, in my morning newspaper I saw that Gurpal Virdi had at last been vindicated by an appeal from an employment tribunal. He had told me that he had felt that he had no option but to test his case against the Metropolitan Police Service in a legal action.

After a lengthy conversation on the rights and wrongs of the Met, I asked what his future plans were. I was staggered when he said: 'Now that I'm cleared of any wrongdoing, I can get back to work again!'

'With the Met?'

'Yes!'

'But', I spluttered in surprise, 'they don't like you there. They don't want you around at all!'

'But that's why I'm going back. By confronting them with the judgment, I hope they will learn the lessons.'

Virdi was so happy in his newly proved integrity, I couldn't bear to puncture his positive mood. I have, sadly, seen too often what happens to police officers from BAME (Black, Asian and other ethnic minority) backgrounds who 'win' in a tribunal, or in some other legal action. Senior white officers seem to feel they have been humiliated.

With Virdi's book now in circulation, there is a written account of institutional racism that I can quote from. Any police officer who claims not to understand the meaning of institutional racism can be directed to *Behind the Blue Line*.

Police services tend to try hard to avoid these cases going to court hearings, preferring to settle out of court, usually with a gagging clause in place and no admission of liability by the Met. Settlements are often double the amount that complainants' lawyers had told them they could expect if they continued with the case until a judgment by the court. What a waste of scarce money!

Little surprise then, that many black British citizens go on, year after year, crying out, 'When will they ever learn?' Such a shame that 'they' – the Association of Chief Police Officers, for example – have never, to my knowledge, done anything to ensure that its members lead on this issue 'from the top'.

Twenty years ago, during the Lawrence Inquiry, we anti-racists noted similarities with the feminist cause. It is un-professional to discriminate against any group of people on the grounds of their sex or colour. It seems, post-Weinstein, that a major change in culture may finally be on the horizon for women. The same is long overdue for BAME people. We are losing many people who could be valuable contributors to the police service.

It is a testament to Virdi's strength of character and the support of his family that he lives not just to tell this important tale but that in conjunction with his excellent legal team of Matt Foot (Birnberg Peirce and Partners) and Henry Blaxland QC (Garden Court Chambers) he put into practice his detective training and gathered evidence that ensured his acquittal.

Thanks to the careful use of official transcripts from his 'retirement case', the reader comes away with the view that Gurpal Virdi's journey in the Metropolitan Police Service was overshadowed by a sinister and potentially orchestrated campaign of terror aimed at destroying the man, his reputation and his career. We are presented with a litany of contentious issues in the UK criminal justice system: the handling of historical sexual assault cases; use of force; racism; police leaking information to the press; inaccurate charging decisions. The overall aim of the campaign was to ensure maximum damage, and the destruction of his new life in local politics, which Virdi had established.

In going forward, we need to understand why this sad state of affairs was allowed to happen. As a panel member of the Macpherson Inquiry, I am concerned that a man who provided cogent and important evidence to the inquiry twenty years ago has been subjected to a catalogue of slurs for which there is no explanation. This has continued throughout his working career and, sadly, even on his retirement.

It is because of this that I am minded to call for the government to commit itself to holding yet another public inquiry to establish what happened and why, so that this does not happen again.

I have to acknowledge that the Stephen Lawrence Inquiry failed to get to the roots of police racism. Of course, there have been huge positive changes in attitudes towards racism. Who would have thought, twenty-five years ago, that Operation Black Vote would be able to boast of achieving fifty-two BAME MPs?

Nonetheless, Gurpal Virdi cannot see enough progress in the police services to warrant moderating the views in his book. What is needed is a radical change in the culture from top to bottom.

Dr Richard Stone was a panel member of the Macpherson Inquiry into the murder of Stephen Lawrence, and has been a lifelong campaigner for social justice.

PROLOGUE

I will never forget Wednesday 15 April 1998. It was a bright, sunny spring day that started like any other. That morning, I had an appointment to take my ten-year-old daughter and seven-year-old son to the dentist for their routine six-month check-up.

I ushered the kids into the car and embarked on the short drive to the dentist. As I pulled out of our residential road and on to the dual carriageway, I sensed something was not quite right. Being surveillance trained, I noticed that an unmarked police car was following me closely and that the man in the passenger seat was talking through a radio, while a marked police car was parked at the nearest bus stop.

As I passed a second roundabout I noticed the blue car was still tailing me so, instead of turning, I went around the roundabout twice, convinced that the car would drive off in a different direction and I could chalk the whole thing down to paranoia. However, the car didn't drive on; it followed me around the roundabout – twice.

Now certain that I was being followed, I drove to the dentist as quickly as possible. After we reached the small side road, adjacent to the clinic, I parked my car. I got out and walked with the kids towards the dentist, which is when I saw a plain-clothes police officer approaching me.

I called my wife, Sathat, and explained that I was being followed by strange men and wanted the children out of the way. She rushed over to collect the children.

In the meantime I went over to the men, who identified themselves as police officers. I was also part of the police force, working as a sergeant with the Met. At the time I had been in the service for sixteen years. They arrested me on the spot for apparently sending racist messages to ethnic minority colleagues at Ealing police station.

What ensued will haunt me for the rest of my life. I was cautioned immediately and escorted home by the officers. I returned to a house that was being searched by a PolSA (Police Search Advisor) team – primarily, PolSA will search properties of those suspected of engaging in terrorist activities. There were officers everywhere; they searched the cars, the drains, the shed, under the carpets, the loft – even my children. Nothing was left unturned: picture frames were taken apart, bathroom fixtures were unscrewed. I felt helpless. I couldn't quite process what was happening – I was in a state of shock. It all seemed so surreal.

They were searching my house for evidence to support their claim that I'd been sending abusive and racist messages. As they searched our kitchen, I thought: 'Are they really expecting to find racist hate mail in a bag of sealed lentils?'

Following a seven-hour search, they left with absolutely

anything and everything. They didn't find any evidence to support their allegations, and after a few months returned most of what they had seized. As the day progressed, I kept telling myself it was all a massive misunderstanding. I knew I hadn't sent abusive messages and was convinced they would realise this when they interviewed me.

• • •

I remember going back to the station one day – it was just before Christmas in 1997 – to check my pigeon hole and finding a printed image of a black man accompanied by the message: 'Not wanted. Keep the police force white so leave now or else', and the initials 'NF' for National Front in the bottom right-hand corner. Twelve Asian and black colleagues at Hanwell and Ealing stations received identical letters. Then, in January, further messages were sent to six black and Asian members of staff working at Ealing station. The police accused me of sending abusive and racist mail to myself and colleagues.

The incident turned into what can only be described as a Kafkaesque nightmare. When I was interviewed by police officers, it became apparent that I'd been away from the office on the days it was alleged that I'd sent the emails from my police computer. However, the Metropolitan Police decided to push forward with the case against me and I was suspended pending an internal disciplinary hearing. Although I was the supposed perpetrator, ethnic minority police employees continued to receive racist mail while I was suspended.

I remained at home until my disciplinary hearing on 7 February 2000. I contested the allegations and maintained my innocence. The hearing ran until 3 March, when I was dismissed from the Met by the Police Discipline Tribunal. It ruled that I had targeted ethnic minority officers and civilian workers after being turned down for promotion.

Deputy Assistant Commissioner Michael Todd, who co-ordinated the investigation, said:

> The ruling is very fair when you look at the effect of what Sergeant Virdi did on his victims, namely those officers who received hate mail and the female officer whom he effectively attempted to frame.
>
> Anyone who sends racist mail is doing something despicable. When it is sent to someone's colleagues, as in this case, it is all the worse.

Todd made this statement to *The Guardian* on 4 March. I was devastated. What about the effects of the Met's actions on me? It had sacked me for a crime I had not committed, and taken away the job I loved. I was determined to fight and prove my innocence once and for all.

I took the Met to an employment tribunal. After a six-week hearing, the tribunal determined that I had been racially discriminated against and I was exonerated. It ruled that I'd been subjected to an entrapment operation: formally interviewed, my house searched, arrested and suspended 'without sufficient evidence to support the allegations'. During the hearing, the evidence indicated that while on duty my conversations with senior officers had been recorded without my knowledge, and on other occasions I had been filmed.

In addition, the tribunal ruled that I had been treated differently to a white female officer, PC Jackie Bachelor, who had also been a suspect. Although Ms Bachelor was said to have been interviewed, her interview was conducted informally – unlike the traumatic experience that I was subjected to. It also later emerged that the police were advised by a forensic psychologist during the hearing. In December 2000, my good friend Paul Foot wrote about the tribunal's findings in *The Guardian*:

> They add up to a devastating attack on police for the way in which they treated Mr Virdi, secretly taped an interview with him, and tried to entrap him in incriminating answers which were not forthcoming for the simple reason that he is an anti-racist, completely innocent of the serious crime alleged against him.

In September 2000, following the outcome of the hearing, I launched an appeal against the findings and sanction of the Police Discipline Tribunal. This appeal was upheld. At a remedy hearing in December 2000, I was awarded damages.

In February 2002, I received a public apology from the then Metropolitan Police Commissioner, Sir John Stevens. Although my wife was against me returning to the Met, I knew I had to go back – I was, and I am still, not the type of person to run away from bullies.

CHAPTER 1

THE LAST DAY

MAY 2012

I want to begin by explaining what happened on Wednesday 9 May 2012 – my last day as a Met officer.

On my way in to work, I stopped by a local newsagent's and bought a copy of *The Independent* to keep me occupied during my hour-long commute. I turned to an article entitled: 'If you complain about racism, your career is finished'. It was an article about me.

• • •

It was a surreal feeling, retiring after thirty years of service. As I walked into the Empress State Building, where I'd been based for the past three years, I felt a mixture of relief and sadness. I had arrived early; it was only 7.45 a.m. when I went to sit down and log on to my computer. A couple of hours later, I received a phone call from my line manager, Inspector David Antoine, who asked me to go upstairs and surrender my warrant card at 4 p.m. It was strictly professional, no small talk, not even a question about how I was feeling on my last day.

All supervising police officers receive daily bulletins listing all press articles featuring the Met. I assumed Inspector Antione had read the bulletin that morning and wondered if that explained his frosty phone call. I looked over at the large windows; it was a grey, rainy day and particularly cold for May. Reflecting on my time with the Met, several thoughts came into my mind.

Back in 1982, I told my parents that I wanted to join the police, but they had been against the idea. I think this was mostly out of fear – London was very different back then. I grew up in Southall, a large suburb in west London. Many of those living in the area were South Asian immigrants; there had been a surge in mass immigration following India's independence in 1947.

In 1979, increasing racial tensions in Southall sparked riots and, notably, the death of teacher and campaigner Blair Peach. An activist campaigning against far right and neo-Nazi organisations, he was killed after attending a demonstration held by the Anti-Nazi League outside Southall town hall on Monday 23 April 1979. Peach and 3,000 others had been protesting a proposed National Front meeting. Although around 2,500 police officers were present, the demonstration soon turned violent, resulting in the death of Peach, who was beaten unconscious by officers in a side street. Public trust in the Met hit a low following the Southall riots, and this feeling was exacerbated in 1981, by the Brixton riots.

Many young black men believed that they were discriminated against by the Met, particularly by the use of the 'Sus Law', which allowed officers to stop and search anyone they deemed suspicious. Distrust culminated in three days of riots – where mostly young black men fought the police, attacked buildings and set fire to vehicles.

It was no surprise, then, that my parents were concerned for my welfare. Despite their protests, I was determined to become a police officer. Injustice and racism had always been important issues to me, and I wanted a career where I could not only protect and serve the public, but also be in a position to make a difference. However, it soon became apparent that my parents were right to be concerned.

On my first night shift, I was patrolling the streets with a colleague in Battersea. We stopped outside a pub called The Chopper, where a car was parked illegally. My partner was writing out a ticket when men suddenly rushed out from the pub and surrounded us, and then proceeded to attack. It was brutal and I still have scars that serve as a reminder of the incident. It later transpired that this pub was known as a favourite haunt of National Front members. I will never forget that evening, and it was no surprise that my parents were less than sympathetic, though still concerned, when I returned home covered in bandages. Attacks are part and parcel of the job, and they never deterred me.

Graduating as a police constable had been tough. I had joined Hendon, the Metropolitan Police training academy, on 10 May 1982 – there were very few ethnic minority trainees during the sixteen-week selection process and I definitely felt that I was treated differently.

Every morning trainees had to parade after breakfast. We were expected to be dressed in full uniform, which would be inspected. I took, and still take, pride in my appearance; I would always make sure my uniform was immaculate. Yet I was constantly singled out and criticised for my shoes, which could always be shinier, or my jacket, which always needed straightening out. Whenever a question was posed during a practical assignment, I would be the first to be called upon for an answer. And, really, none of this bothered me – I took it all in my stride – any criticism would help me become a better officer, and that was the only reason I was there. Nothing else mattered.

My passing-out parade after graduating from the academy remains one of my proudest moments. We were allowed to invite family members to come and watch the ceremony, so I asked my father, mother, brother, sister-in-law and nephew. I felt great; I was in the best physical shape I'd ever been in and had passed all my tests. I could not wait to start my first shift.

• • •

Until the events of 1998, I'd had an unblemished career in uniformed, CID and specialist squads. After completing my probation, I joined the District Support Unit (DSU) in order to challenge myself. It required further training; we had to learn how to carry and wield a large plastic shield. Being part of the DSU also meant working in the more challenging parts of south and central London, and I also patrolled during the 1984 miners' strike. But although the DSU was a great place to learn, I soon realised that I preferred the investigative aspects of police work.

So, after my time with the DSU was up, I applied to join the crime squad. It was notoriously difficult to get into the crime squad, but I had an excellent record to recommend me and I joined officially in 1985. This was followed by a stint with the SO11 squad, which dealt with intelligence surveillance and was based at Scotland Yard – eventually it became the National Crime Intelligence Service (NCIS). In 1992, after a promotion to sergeant, I became a uniformed officer at Ealing, where I spent the next six years before being accused of sending racist hate mail.

After my reinstatement and return to work in 2002, I was targeted several times by the police force. Not only did they try again to blame me for the hate mail, I was also criticised for reporting officers for drinking on duty and all my promotion applications were rejected. Whenever I told Sathat, my wife, she always said: 'What did you expect? Your file has been marked for ever.' She was right – my career effectively ended in 1998. However, there is no point in dwelling on what could have been.

The retirement process had been relatively straightforward. I had submitted the paperwork in March and this was followed by a two-week handover period. On my last day all I had to do was hand in my warrant card, which I had carried with me for thirty years. Despite it being my last day, I had still received several emails, many of them from members of the public and other police officers who had been victims of inequality. Midway through the morning, I received an interview request from Guy Smith at BBC London News – he was keen to interview me.

I met Guy, who I'd known for several years, outside West Brompton train station and we went to a nearby café during my lunch break. Guy ordered our teas and we sat down at a table while the BBC crew set up for the interview. The recorded clip made it into the afternoon and evening BBC London News bulletins.

'Racism is still a major problem within Britain's largest police service: that is the conclusion of this man, Detective Sergeant Gurpal Virdi. This afternoon, his final day after thirty years with the Met, he hands in his warrant card,' reported Guy.

'Ethnic officers, if they raise their head above the parapet, are targeted, disciplined, criminalised, given bad publicity which never used to happen before but now is happening,' I responded.

Guy continued: 'Sergeant Virdi, a Sikh officer, joined the Met in 1982 … He had an unblemished career until 1997, when racist hate mail was sent to ethnic minority officers based in Ealing. Sergeant Virdi was arrested and then sacked but an employment tribunal later found him innocent and he was reinstated. He was awarded compensation…'

The interview lasted half an hour. I told Guy that when I left the Met in 2012, I would be only the twelfth ethnic minority officer to have 'survived' and have completed thirty years of service. It was an abysmal, shameful record: London's ethnic population totalled just over 40 per cent in 2011, yet only 9 per cent of Met officers came from an ethnic minority background. Admittedly, this was a marked improvement from when I had joined in 1982.

Back then, only 0.2 per cent of officers came from an ethnic minority background, which translated into approximately 150 of us. I really believed that the number of ethnic minority officers should have been higher. I also told Guy I'd not been offered an exit interview.

When I got back from lunch, I was met with a flurry of voicemails. People had seen Guy's lunchtime news report and had left supportive messages. But I also had a message from a Superintendent Smith, telling me to contact him immediately. When I dialled his number, he said he wanted to conduct an exit interview. I refused. It is usual procedure that when police officers and employees retire or leave to join another organisation, an exit interview is conducted a week before the employee's leaving date. For me, this did not happen. I can only assume that Smith had seen my interview with Guy and as a result had contacted me to offer an exit interview.

Colleagues approached my desk to ask why I was still in the office. Someone wondered why I wasn't throwing a party to celebrate, while someone else asked why a senior officer hadn't taken me out for lunch. Members of my team had taken me for lunch the day before, but nobody, including my line manager, had done anything to celebrate my retirement.

It was almost time to surrender my warrant card. I couldn't help feeling sad. I walked over to Inspector Antoine's desk, and we made small talk for about thirty seconds. Then I handed him my warrant card, and he said: 'Thanks.' I waited for him to say something else, but he didn't, so I asked if he would be escorting me out. He said security would show me out.

How embarrassing, I thought. He couldn't even be bothered to walk me out of the building – which was usual practice.

'Is this it? Does the Head of Department, Denise Milani, want to say anything to me?'

'She is very busy and cannot see you. There is another officer who is being given a retirement function next week. You can collect your certificate of service then.'

I couldn't quite believe my own ears. I looked him in the eye.

'Just post it to my home address. I've left something on my desk that I need to collect, and one of my team members can escort me out.'

I walked away – in equal parts humiliated and disgusted by his behaviour.

I asked a colleague, Ibrar Ahmed, if I could make calls on his phone, and he happily obliged. I was lucky to have made good friends at the Met, and I asked if they would escort me out. Despite all that had happened over the past fourteen years, I still loved the job, and I didn't want my last day to end with me being escorted from the building by security.

At about 4.30 p.m., a group of ten of us – all ethnic minority officers – left together. It was a wonderful feeling to leave alongside officers I could call friends; they were proof I hadn't been alone. As I walked through the security gate, I still harboured no regrets about my return to the force in 2002. I left with my head held high, proud of making a stand against inequality, corruption and bad practices.

CHAPTER 2

A NEW BEGINNING

On the afternoon of 11 August 2011, I logged into my email account and saw I had a new message: I had been nominated as a London 2012 torchbearer through the 'Moment to Shine' campaign. I would now be reviewed by one of twelve regional selection panels who were seeking 2,012 individuals with the most inspirational stories of personal achievement and/or contribution to the community. If successful, I would have a chance to be one of the 8,000 torchbearers for the Olympic torch relay.

What an honour! Just receiving the nomination filled me with joy. It was a great feeling to be recognised for everything I had achieved, both in terms of standing up to racism in the Met and for my voluntary work in the community. On 16 March 2012, which also happened to be my son's twenty-first birthday, I was officially informed that I'd been selected as an Olympic torchbearer. I was ecstatic.

The day I carried the torch, 24 July, is another day I will never forget. I would be responsible for bringing the torch from Richmond, over Kew Bridge, to Hounslow, my local area. Hundreds of people from the local community had made their way to the bridge. As I prepared to receive the torch from the previous runner, I was full of excitement and anticipation.

As I started running, I was overwhelmed by all the cheering and flag-waving from adults and small children lining the sides of the road. I spotted my uncle and aunt in the crowd; despite living in Canada, they had made the trip to London to cheer me on and them being there was a wonderful surprise. After finishing my part of the route, I was out of breath but happy. Being part of something so special was helping me to let go of the past, and enabling me to move forward with my life.

Prior to the race, my wife and I had booked an area at a local pub, for a mini celebration. We wanted to thank our friends and family who had come to watch me run. We also invited local residents, who told me how proud they were that one of their own was bringing the torch to Hounslow.

My participation in the Olympic relay was covered by the local press. As a result of the publicity, an online hate campaign began against me and I was made aware of its existence by a journalist. I wanted to know who had started the campaign, and when I asked the journalist he told me that it was employees of the Met. I made a complaint to the Met, but it was decided that no action would be taken against them. This response did not surprise me.

● ● ●

Although I'd retired from the force, I wanted to continue working for the local community. So, in September 2012, I signed up to a thirteen-week City & Guilds course called 'Preparing to Teach in the Lifelong Learning Sector' (PTLLS). I also applied for a paid job as a Linkline officer with an organisation called Hounslow Homes. My role involved responding to the needs of vulnerable people in the community, and I enjoyed the work, as it allowed me to use the skills and knowledge I'd developed as a police officer. Towards the end of 2012, I successfully completed my PTTLS course.

I had one other keen interest and that was politics, particularly local politics. I wanted to ensure residents in the local community received the representation they deserved. I wanted to clean up the roads and boost local investment. I wanted to make a real and tangible difference. As an independent member of the Standards Committee, I was also very aware of the corruption and bad practices that existed in some parts of the council.

In early 2012, I joined the Labour Party. There were several reasons why I joined Labour, but the main one was my father – he had always been a supporter. During the hate mail case, he had persuaded friends in the Labour Party to sign a petition on my behalf that they then submitted to then Metropolitan Police Commissioner Sir Paul Condon. Watching my father and his friends standing in a line outside Tintagel House, Vauxhall, almost every day, with placards reading 'Gurpal Virdi is innocent', are moments I will never forget.

Soon after joining the Labour Party, I found out about its Future Candidate Programme. I'd never heard of the programme, but as I read through the documentation and the pledge that it was designed to help people from all backgrounds and experiences to become politicians, I was convinced that this would help me achieve my vision of contributing positive changes within the community. I submitted an application for this programme in October 2012. My application proved successful.

The programme started in January 2013 at Sheffield. It was a particularly cold winter that year, and as the day arrived for me to travel up to Sheffield, the snow was falling thick and fast. Sathat did not want me to drive in such treacherous weather conditions, so I looked up whether I could reach Sheffield by train. Unfortunately the weather had affected the service and there were several cancellations and delays. I was determined to attend the programme, however, so at around 4 p.m. that afternoon, I set off for Sheffield, much against Sathat's wishes. I should have listened to her.

On approaching Sheffield, I hit black ice and my car skidded and sped out of control. Knowing that an accident could be fatal for myself and other drivers, I drove onto the adjacent grass verge. But I was unable to regain control of the car and ended up crashing into a large tree.

Not to sound too dramatic, but I honestly thought that that was it. By some miracle, when I opened my eyes I was OK. I got out of the car and knew instantly there was no way I would be able to drive it again – the front of it had absorbed the impact of the crash and saved my life. Nevertheless, and despite this horrific accident, I was determined to do the course. I stood for over four hours waiting for roadside assistance to take the car to a garage and me to the hotel.

The course was illuminating. The training provided me with the practical skills and knowledge I so desperately needed in order to take the next big step – putting myself forward as a local councillor. We were provided with an overview of the selection processes that were in place, told how to build a campaigning team and how to run a successful election campaign.

I met potential candidates from a diverse range of backgrounds and experiences. Many candidates were on the course because they wanted to become Members of Parliament (MPs), but I was only interested in becoming a councillor. Being selected for the programme had boosted my confidence; I felt that I had the skills and knowledge required to be a successful councillor. To have faith in myself was important to me. After being reinstated to the Met, I had applied for promotion several times, but each time got rejected. I tried to understand why: I would ask for feedback, and try to learn from my mistakes. The constant rejection meant that at times I doubted myself. Perhaps I really wasn't good enough. In a way the course saved me by reminding me I was capable, and it felt wonderful to know other people believed in me too.

A few months after the programme finished, I took the first step to becoming a local councillor. I submitted my application to the Labour Party for a spot on the coveted selection list. A few weeks later I received a letter informing me my application had been successful, and I was required to attend an interview in Hounslow.

The interview was relatively straightforward. The panel asked why I wanted to become a councillor; what relevant experience I had; what work I'd done in the local community; and what I knew about the selection process. It was also an opportunity to learn more about the role – they told me what the job entailed and warned I could be working all sorts of hours. I found out the next day that I had made the list.

Around the same time, I was invited to a Future Candidates Programme meeting hosted by my mentor, Sadiq Khan MP, now Mayor of London. The meeting was in an office block by St James's Park Tube station, near New Scotland Yard. It felt weird being back. There must have been fifteen or so people at the meeting. I glanced across the room and saw a man staring at me. When our eyes met he looked away quickly, but I recognised him. I couldn't recall his name, but I was sure he'd been on a police operation with me during my time at Scotland Yard. It was obvious he didn't want to speak to me, so I shrugged it off and turned to speak with another candidate.

Five minutes must have passed before the man, who had been quietly keeping an eye on me, approached and started making conversation.

'Don't I know you from somewhere? What are you doing here?'

I didn't want to give too much away, so I just told him I was interested in politics. I have to admit I was quite suspicious, so I thought it would be best to ask him which cohort he belonged to (the Labour Party usually runs a couple of Future Candidate Programmes throughout the year). He told me he hadn't attended any of the programmes. Why was he there then? And why engage in small talk with me?

I'm known for being quite blunt, so I looked him in the face and said, half-jokingly and half-seriously: 'Look, you need to ensure you are briefed properly by your superiors before you attend these events; am I your target for today?' He did not respond – he just smiled and walked away.

As he headed towards the door, I suddenly remembered who he was. We had worked together on a surveillance operation – he was a Special Branch officer. The Special Branch is a unit in the Met that focuses on acquiring and developing intelligence. This intelligence is usually of a political nature and officers use this information to conduct investigations – to protect the state from perceived threats of subversion. The officer hadn't even stayed for Sadiq Khan's speech.

CHAPTER 3

WASIM ANQKAR

WASIM ANQKAR'S
INTERVIEW MARCH 2013

In January 2013, a man named Wasim Anqkar visited two south London police stations, Brixton and Kennington. He wanted to file a complaint against the Met. On both occasions, he was turned away and told that he would need to speak to a superintendent.

Following his unsuccessful visits, Anqkar obtained a telephone number for Sapphire – a Metropolitan Police unit made up of specialist officers who investigate claims of sexual assault and violence – and made contact. According to a Crime Reporting Information System (CRIS) report, Sapphire contacted the Directorate of Professional Standards (DPS), the body responsible for investigating complaints against the professional conduct of Met officers. The DPS advised Anqkar that he could speak with officers at any police station in London.

On 13 March 2013, Anqkar spoke with officers at Tabor

Grove, Wimbledon. A taped interview was conducted by PC Kevin Newton and lasted one hour and forty-two minutes, followed by a formal written statement. Newton worked for Sapphire's SC&02 team, which deals with child protection. Another detective constable, Claire Hastings, was sat in an adjacent room, where she was watching the interview on a monitor and taking notes. Prior to the interview, DC Hastings had carried out background checks on Anqkar, establishing his date of birth as 29 August 1970. She also contacted the DPS intelligence desk with a view to identifying any possible suspects, and was called in to speak to Anqkar as he wanted to report a crime of sexual assault that occurred in 1987.

PC Newton starts the interview by asking Anqkar to confirm his name and to tell him everything he remembers about the incident in as much detail as possible.

Anqkar begins by telling Newton that he cannot remember the exact date of the alleged sexual assault. He'd only recently been reminded of the incident when, as an employment requirement for a job as a driver, he had obtained a criminal record bureau (CRB) check. When the results of the CRB check had come through, he had noticed a conviction for possession of a dangerous weapon in 1987 and thought: 'Wow! That's a blast from the past.'

Anqkar alleges that at the time of the incident he was living at home with his parents on Brussels Road, Battersea. He had been completing a work experience placement, where he had been carrying out dry-lining and plastering for a local tradesman. He would often carry his tools with him to and from work. On this particular day, he was on his way back from work, when he bumped into a friend of his, Michael, whom he had known for years. While the two boys were chatting, Anqkar's neighbour Denzel approached them.

According to Anqkar, Denzel told the boys to 'fuck off', prompting Anqkar to pull a knife from his pocket. When asked about the knife during the interview, Anqkar recalls that it was a Stanley knife, one with a straight edge that he used to cut plasterboard. He had also been carrying other tools, including a hammer, which all belonged to the trades-man that he was working for. Anqkar demanded Denzel stop bullying him, before running down St John's Hill. PC Newton probed Anqkar for more information about Michael, but Anqkar was unable to provide even a surname, stating that they are no longer in contact.

Initially, Anqkar does not provide the interviewers with any context for the altercation between himself and Denzel, but when probed further during the interview he claims that he felt like he was being backed into a corner by Denzel, which is why he pulled the knife out of his pocket.

PC Newton is interested in finding out more about Denzel and asks Anqkar about him. Anqkar recalls that Denzel never liked him as a kid. He remembers being part of a latchkey youth club, and every year, at the end of the summer holidays, the club would have a party for the kids up to the ages of fifteen and sixteen. According to Anqkar, Denzel used to attend the summer party because he was in-terested in one of the women that looked after the children, and that Anqkar and the other kids would snigger and laugh as he was 'sniffing around her and all that'.

Anqkar goes on to claim that he was attacked by Denzel on two occasions, the first assault occurring when Anqkar was around ten years old. Anqkar explains that he put the attack down to Denzel's sexual frustration. PC Newton asks Anqkar if he told anyone about Denzel's bullying, to which Anqkar replies that he did tell his parents, but that his dad didn't do anything about it, before going on to say: 'I'm ashamed to say this, but he was a coward.'

Anqkar goes on to recall being stopped by two plain-clothes police officers following his altercation with Denzel.

> They grabbed me and they say: 'Right, you are under arrest, what's it, wait here, yeah.' You know, the knife was produced out of my pocket, I handed in the knife, OK. They went and spoke to the other guy, the other guy that was involved in it and he said: 'Ah, I don't want to press charges…'

When asked who told Anqkar that he was under arrest, he claims that it was an officer called George. It is worth noting that Anqkar states quite clearly that the altercation between himself and Denzel occurred at the top of St John's Hill, after which he ran down the hill and was met by the police officers. This is important as Anqkar claims that while George places him under arrest, Tom, another officer, speaks with Denzel.

Anqkar then claims that they all waited for a Sherpa van

to arrive. Anqkar does not remember either officer calling for a van, but one arrived and he was placed in the back. He was not handcuffed. He describes the van as white and old-fashioned, with a blue light, two double doors and benches on either side.

'I was handcuffed when I got into the van … the van door gets shut, yeah, and now my back is towards the back doors and that is when I get handcuffed.'

When asked about how this happens, Anqkar confirms that George is standing in front of him and has handcuffed him to the front. Anqkar describes the handcuffs as old-fashioned, with a chain in-between the cuffs, forcing his palms to face together. George then asks Anqkar for his name and Anqkar replies: 'Harry Anqkar.'

Anqkar goes on to provide the following account of what happened in the van:

He's pulled his hand back straight away, just came as a total surprise, slapped me straight in the face, a downward slap, really powerful slap, really powerful, blaf, straight in the face. 'What kind of name is that for a nigger?' And that's where it started…

Now he's slapped me in the face, OK, I've gone down, he's tried to grab me by the neck. But I've had some train-ing in, what's it, in self-defence, so I, so what's it, what I do is if I feel threated I always pull my neck in, pull my neck into my, onto my shoulder, I've been taught that. So now he is trying to get me in a headlock in the back of his van, OK, but he can't get me in a headlock. He can't get me in a headlock that will subdue me 'cos he can't get my windpipe, yeah?

So he's kicking and punching, kneeing me, you know, trying to get me to allow him to have me in a headlock. I'm now allowing him to do that. I'm being thrown around the van, from side to side … All I was doing is growling and puffing and panting and just trying to make as much noise as possible, you understand, you know, the van must have been shaking from side to side. 'Cos I was banging off that wall, I was banging off this wall…

This is going on for a—it seemed like ten, fifteen minutes but, you know, really and truly was only, it's got to be, you know, it had to be under a minute, OK? … The other officer who was there, his name was Tom, as soon as this started, OK, for the first, I'd say for the first ten seconds, he kept quiet, but he saw it was going too far. He saw that, you know, I was gonna be, either I was gonna be really badly hurt and he started protesting there and then, screaming and shouting…

PC Newton then asks Anqkar if he can use the exact words that were used by Tom inside the van. He told officers what he remembered: "'Fucking stop it, George, fucking you're killing him. Leave him alone. Fuck's sake, George, why are you doing this?' Screaming and shouting at the top of his voice, you understand? The only thing he didn't do was physically get involved and actually pull George off me.'

When probed further about Tom's role in the incident, Anqkar gave the following information about a man that he had only just met: 'I know Tom wasn't in the force for very long and I know he's an educated man as well, you understand.'

Anqkar claims he was then thrown to the floor, before being pulled up.

> George was sitting on the floor with his feet on my shoulders and pulling my handcuffs … 'Are you gonna stop? Why aren't you gonna give up?' I said: 'I'm not doing anything to give up,' you understand? Screaming and shouting he was. And then what he done, OK, he turned me over onto my side, yeah, turned me over onto my side, sat across my back, yeah, and got his truncheon, yeah, and stuck it up my arse, you understand? Now as this truncheon's gone up my, I was totally surprised. I didn't, I wasn't expecting anything like this, I, I wasn't expecting a beating, yeah? Got this truncheon, stuck up my arse, yeah, and started pushing it up and down.

When questioned further about this in the interview, Anqkar claims that he was rolled onto his left-hand side with his arms pulled in. When asked about the truncheon, he recalls: 'It was a collapsible truncheon, you understand, a small one like this that [gestures with his hands], then it came, it, it was quite long.'

PC Newton asks Anqkar about what he was wearing. He recalls that he was wearing a pair of shell bottoms, very thin with a lining and pants underneath. When asked whether his trousers were torn or damaged, Anqkar provides a vivid account of what happened to him and gives PC Newton the following answer: 'To be honest I can't remember, d'you know what I mean, I cannot remember if anything was split, torn or whatever, I can't.'

Anqkar then goes on to explain what happened after he had been assaulted with the truncheon:

> Now the pain was so bad, yeah, I moved a bit further down to the van doors by this time and I had quite a bit of a, you know, like a leverage, yeah, so as he was doing it, I was kicking the doors, 'cos there was nothing else I could do. I was kicking the doors, kicking the doors, kicking the doors and bang, the van door flew open. Now as the van doors flew open, you understand, the van doors flew open at [the] beginning of Falcon Road, Clapham Junction.

Anqkar describes how, as the van doors flew open, he could see that there was a bus stop as they were driving past. He then claims that Tom started to bang on the wooden partition in the van, attempting to get the driver to stop. When asked whether he believes the driver could see into the back of the van, Anqkar tells Newton that he does not think so. Something tells him that there was a small window, but all he can confirm is that there is a wood partition between the driver and the back of the van.

According to Anqkar, upon hearing the banging, the van

driver then stopped, ran to the back of the van and shut the doors. He then goes on to describe how George pulls him up and sits Anqkar down, and how he was now feeling flinchy and nervous. He then says:

> 'I can't believe that you would do that to a fifteen-year-old boy.' And they went: 'What, fifteen? What's your fucking date of birth. What's your date of birth?' I said: '29 August 1970. I'm fifteen, I'm on, what's it, I'm on work experience.' That's when they sort of like looked at each other, you understand?

He confirms throughout the interview, several times in fact, that he was fifteen at the time of this incident. This is until PC Newton probes Anqkar about the CRB check he referred to at the start of the interview:

> PC NEWTON: 'Is, in … 1987 is that when you think, you're fifteen…'
> W ANQKAR: 'Mmm.'
> PC NEWTON: 'Sorry, your date of birth is 1970.'
> W ANQKAR: 'Yeah.'
> PC NEWTON: 'And if you're, sorry, that's going to be 1985 then.'
> W ANQKAR: 'Oh yeah, right, '85, yeah. Mmm.'

Throughout the interview, Anqkar stated that he was fifteen at the time of the incident. The CRB check, which he told police officers had reminded him of the assault, had confirmed that he was convicted in 1987 for carrying a Stanley knife.

Anqkar gives conflicting accounts of what happened after he arrived at Battersea police station. Initially, he states that both George and Tom opened the doors of the van and escorted him up the stairs to the charge room, where they were met with a custody sergeant sitting alone. When probed about this again, he states that he cannot remember whether it was the driver or George and Tom that opened the van doors once they arrived at the station, due to being so frightened. PC Newton asks Anqkar to provide a sketch of the layout of Battersea police station, but when I asked to see his drawing, the Met claimed that it had gone missing.

Anqkar explains that he provided a custody sergeant with his personal details, including his name and date of birth, before handing over everything he was carrying to the sergeant. He is then asked to go to a police cell, but Anqkar remembers refusing, as he remembered from TV programmes that he had watched that this was not standard procedure: suspects were always escorted to a cell by a police officer. The sergeant demands again that Anqkar goes to a cell and gives him clear instructions on where to go and Anqkar acquiesces.

As he approaches the cell, he recalls that he sees George and Tom by the cell that he is supposed to be going into and describes them as 'growling [he growls], you know, fists clenched, both of them, you know what I mean, growling, you know, like intimidating, you know...'

He then explains that he charged towards George and Tom, managing to catch them both off guard, before the officers turned to grab him in an attempt to pull him out of the cell that he has run into. George and Tom managed to pull off his jacket when they tried to do this, before shutting the door to the cell.

Anqkar says that he does not see George and Tom for three or four hours, by which time Anqkar's father has arrived to collect him from the police station. He claims that there was no interview at the time, and that his father was standing in the waiting room ready to take Anqkar home, and after they left the station they travelled by bus to their home.

When asked if Anqkar told his father about the incident, he confirmed that he did: 'I said "Dad, they stuck the truncheon up my arse." He was [like]: "Just shut up, just shut up. Come on. Come on." And that was it.'

Following the incident, Anqkar states that he was required to attend Balham Juvenile Court for the arrest. He attended court without his family members and went with only his friends. When asked if he had any legal representation, he confirmed he was represented by a 'little Indian lady' and that he did not disclose to her at any point during the trial or meetings what had happened to him. He recalls that George gave evidence at the trial, but that Tom had left the force two weeks after the incident. He is not asked how he knew that Tom Makins had left the force. Anqkar was found guilty of possession of a knife, and was fined. He claimed during the interview that this was his first experience of being in trouble with the police, and that he had not had any encounters prior to this incident.

Throughout the interview, Anqkar refers to me as George. When asked about 'George' in the interview, Anqkar states that 'his real name is PC, DC, Virdi Girdi. George is his nickname. George is what his people call him. His name is Virdi Girdi.'

At this point in the interview, upon hearing this name, PC Newton unexpectedly leaves the room. He tells Anqkar that he needs to have a quick chat with his colleague Claire.

When Anqkar was asked what he was thinking after he had been assaulted, he said the following:

> Shock. You know, shock, dirty bastard, shock, can't believe it. What hit my mind was Mannering ... They used to do, put people under manners years ago, we used to watch it on films, you know, old-fashioned films like in Borstal, you understand ... that was the sort of thing that used to happen in children's homes when there was rival, rivalry in children's homes ... To, you know, to control his mind...

As PC Newton starts wrapping up the interview, DC Hastings, who has been watching the entire interview, walks into the room and asks perhaps the most important question: 'I just want to ask one more thing: why have you decided to come and see us now?'

Anqkar takes no time to respond:

[The reason] I've decided to come and see you now is that, you know, people are listening, do you understand? You know, you've got people, this man is not, well hopefully he is not dead ... you've got other cases, Jimmy Savile, everyone comes out when they die, do you understand, you know? I want to get him alive, you know, when he's alive he can pay for what he's done to me. Hopefully the man still works for the Met, you understand?

The first person that's told me that was rape was the police officer that I give the first interview to. I thought it was just sexual assault. You understand?

When you do get hold of George ... I know George, he will deny, he won't take it [a lie detector test] because he knows that it'll be more of a guilty, you know what I mean?

CHAPTER 4

A KNOCK ON
THE DOOR

I spent late 2013 and early 2014 preparing for the local elections that would be taking place in May 2014. I had been selected by Labour Party members as the official candidate for Cranford and this meant attending several weekend courses on what being a councillor entailed, as well as learning more about the structure of the Labour Party.

My work with the local community also kept me busy. In the lead-up to Christmas, there had been an unusually high number of burglaries in Cranford. As a result, many residents had dropped by the house to complain about the lack of action from police officers. I could sense that the community was dissatisfied with the way the police were handling incidents, and their resentment and distrust were growing; I wanted to do something to remediate this increasingly widespread feeling. Therefore, in collaboration with other concerned residents, we set up a 'Residents Group'. The group was headed up by a lady, Janet Stevens; Sathat was appointed deputy chair and I was named as general secretary.

We were an instant success. Our first meeting took place

at the local church hall, and attendees included both local residents and police officers from Hounslow police station. Locals were able to put their questions and concerns to the police, who were not given an easy time. The meeting helped ease the mounting tension and, more importantly, I noticed there was a renewed sense of confidence in the police amongst the residents – I was pleased.

By early February, I was preparing for the local elections, working as a Linkline officer and trying to initiate as many community improvement projects as possible, but I still felt I had more to give. It was around this time that I came across an ad asking for volunteer panel members for the Community Youth Offending Panel. Youth offender panels are a unique way of dealing with young people who commit offences. Panels are borough-wide and made up of members of the community who encourage young offenders to take responsibility for their actions, while also guiding and helping them as adults to change their behaviour for good. Young offenders are given a platform to speak about their own experiences and many discuss the impact of committing a crime and the help they need in order to prevent them reoffending in the future.

I applied straight away. I had worked with troubled youths in the past and this seemed like the perfect role for me, as it would allow me to call on my experience as both a police and family liaison officer. My application was successful and, following an interview, I was invited to start the necessary training. I began sitting on panels right away – initially as an observer and eventually as a fully fledged panel member.

Although 2014 had only just begun, it was already looking good – until I received a knock on my door on 25 March 2014.

● ● ●

I opened the front door that morning and found two men in suits, who introduced themselves as detective constables David Gadsby and Jon Payne. I invited them in, believing that they had come to discuss an allegation made by Hounslow Council's Standards Committee, of which I was an independent member.

'So what can I do to help you, officers?' I asked.

Gadsby replied that they had come to read me a letter. I was slightly confused, but gestured for them to continue. Gadsby took the letter from his inside pocket and started to read:

Dear Mr Virdi

A historic allegation has been made to the Metropolitan Police Service which may concern you.

The alleged incident is said to have occurred in 1986 and is said to relate to you assaulting a prisoner whilst you were on duty.

It is intended to interview you with regards to this allegation.

You are being given a period of seven days to elect a convenient date and time for an interview to be conducted.

Once a mutually agreeable time is set I would ask that you attend Heathrow police station where disclosure will be provided and an interview under caution will be conducted. Should you wish to be legally represented the disclosure document will be provided to your representative.

As indicated above, at this point in time, it is not intended to arrest you, however I must remind you that should you not comply with the request, as outlined above, the situation will change.

At this point in time I cannot answer any questions regarding the complaint or the allegation but can assure you that prior to the interview taking place disclosure will be provided.

I will now ask you to sign this document to confirm that I have read the contents to you and that I have provided you a copy.

Yours sincerely

Detective Constable David Gadsby

As he read out the letter, I knew immediately that a mistake had been made – I had never assaulted a prisoner. However, I felt extremely uneasy; a false accusation levelled against me felt all too familiar.

Gadsby handed me a copy of the letter and asked me to sign it, acknowledging that I understood what it said. It was all very formal and matter of fact. I assumed that our conversation was being taped, as they had been in the past, so I remained calm and polite. I asked Gadsby: 'Why is the interview at Heathrow? Why not Hounslow police station, my local station?'

'It has been decided to be conducted at Heathrow.'

This was ridiculous. Whatever this was, I just wanted it resolved as soon as possible.

'Look, shall we do this now? I'm free for the next few hours and keen to sort this out now.'

'No, not today; the interview will take place within seven days as it states in the letter.'

As helpful as ever then, I thought.

'OK, fine. This means I will need to inform my employers and request time off,' I said.

They left the house, and as the front door shut behind them, my head was spinning – I was stunned. What on earth were the police playing at? I tried to think back to 1986, but had no idea what I was doing twenty-eight years ago. Who on earth would make such an allegation? Was this another witch hunt? Why couldn't the police leave me and my family alone? I had done everything by the book; I'd certainly never assaulted anyone. I couldn't help but wonder if this had something to do with my foray into politics. Was this an attempt at silencing me? I could feel my blood pressure rising and felt suddenly out of breath. I had to tell myself that I was getting worked up for no reason – this was a mistake, plain and simple; there could be no other explanation.

●　●　●

With only two months to go until the local elections, I had planned to go campaigning with fellow Labour Party members that afternoon, but my morning visitors had rattled me and I called and cancelled. First, I would have to deal with what had just happened.

I tried to think logically about the best course of action to take. If this was going to be a repeat of the racist hate mail case, I would need legal help. I reread the letter. It stated that the alleged incident had taken place while I was on duty. I looked up a number for the Police Federation, a national staff association that represents the interests of police officers up to the rank of chief inspector.

I dialled the number but no one picked up, so I left a voice message asking someone to call back as soon as possible. I followed up my call with an email that same day, and received a swift reply from the federation stating that the matter had been passed to the sergeant's board. Until I had more information, I wasn't quite sure what to do next.

Sathat had been working that day. When she returned home, she immediately sensed something was up.

'What's wrong?' she asked. 'You look like you've had a tough day.'

I told her what had happened.

'Well, it's got to be a mistake, you've never assaulted anyone! And why has this person come forward now? It's been over twenty-eight years – come on, it's ridiculous.'

She told me not to worry and we decided not to tell the children; after all, we were still convinced that it was all a mistake. But, despite Sathat appearing outwardly confident, I could tell the same thought was going through her mind: what if history was repeating itself?

The next day I received a call from the Police Federation; they had assigned me a solicitor who would accompany me to my police interview. I also asked if they could get in touch with the Directorate of Police Standards as soon as possible, to ask if our interview could be moved from Heathrow to Hounslow. I wanted the matter cleared up quickly. The federation rep got back to me an hour later to let me know that the interview would take place the next day at Hounslow police station.

On the morning of 27 March, I woke up feeling uneasy and anxious. I had learnt from past experience that with the Met you should always expect the unexpected. As I was leaving the house, Sathat walked me to the door, gave me a hug and said: 'Don't worry about it – I'm sure it's all a massive misunderstanding. Keep calm.'

When I arrived at the station, I was introduced to my solicitor, Dalia Naaman. She was from Reynolds Dawson Solicitors, a firm based in Charing Cross. She asked me what I knew about the disclosure. I replied: 'Apart from the letter Gadsby read out to me on Tuesday, I have no idea.'

'I know who you are, I'm aware of your history with the Met Police. I think this allegation is highly suspicious,' she said.

I could not agree more. Soon after, Gadsby appeared and called Ms Naaman into a private office. I was asked to take a seat in the waiting room. I assumed that Ms Naaman was receiving further disclosure regarding the allegation.

After about ten minutes of me pacing up and down in the waiting room, Ms Naaman emerged from the office. She held a single piece of paper – it was indeed further disclosure.

Then we were escorted to the room where I would be interviewed. Ms Naaman and I were given time alone before the interview to discuss the disclosure and new information that she had just received in her discussion with the police. The interview room was windowless and cramped and had been prepped for an official interview to take place. We sat side by side. Ms Naaman produced the A4 piece of paper she'd been given by officers, and reminded me that I would be interviewed under caution, and not arrest. She read from the paper:

An allegation has been made by Mr Wasim Anqkar that in October 1986 he was stopped and arrested by PC Virdi. Mr Anqkar states that PC Virdi knew him as he had stopped and spoken to him prior to this incident on several occasions.

Mr Anqkar was fifteen years of age in 1986. He used the first name Harry. Mr Anqkar knew PC Virdi as George.

Mr Anqkar was in possession of a knife and as a result was arrested. He was handcuffed and placed in the rear of a police vehicle. Mr Anqkar describes the vehicle as a Sherpa van with a wooden partition between the driver and wooden bench seating on each side of the van. Mr Anqkar could not see the van driver as the partition blocked his view. There was no passenger in the passenger seat.

It is said PC Virdi slapped Mr Anqkar in the face before attempting to put him in a headlock; he was punched and kicked to the ground. PC Virdi held him on the floor and sat on him. Mr Anqkar was on his side. PC Virdi then forced an item into his bottom. This item was forced into his bottom through his loose-fitting running trousers and boxer shorts.

The attack stopped after this. Mr Anqkar was taken to Battersea police station and charged with the offensive weapon matter.

He did not disclose the attack to police at the time. He's been asked why it's taken him so many years to report the allegation. He's stated that it's only recently that he considers allegations such as this one are listened to.

It took me a couple of minutes to come to terms with what Ms Naaman had just read out to me. Who on earth was this Mr Anqkar, and why was he accusing me of such a horrific crime? It was also the first time that I was made aware of the date on which the alleged incident had apparently occurred – October 1986.

'Do you know Anqkar? Can you recall the incident?' Ms Naaman asked me.

'I cannot recall him at all, and the incident definitely did not happen,' I said. 'I can't remember the incident because it never happened.'

'Well, I think you should do a "no comment" interview.'

I flatly refused – there was no way I was going to give a 'no comment' interview. I knew I was innocent – I wanted to talk and protest my innocence.

'No chance,' I replied, 'I want to conduct the interview and speak to Gadsby. I have nothing to hide. I want to get to the bottom of this and I want to understand why the Metropolitan Police insist on harassing me!'

She listened to my response and then suggested again that I did a 'no comment' statement. Again, I refused.

All I knew about my supposed crime was what was written on that single piece of paper – I had no idea on what day the alleged incident had occurred; I had no idea whether or not I was on duty when the allegation was made; I did not even know where the incident was supposed to have happened. How could anyone expect me to make a statement, even if it was only a 'no comment' statement, when I had so little information? All I could do was go into the interview and maintain that I had never assaulted anyone while on duty.

As soon as we had finished our discussion, the two interviewing officers – DC Gadsby and DC Payne – walked in and sat down. It seemed odd to me that DC Payne had known exactly when Ms Naaman and I had finished our discussion. Anyway, I was ready. It was 11.45 a.m., and it was time to get to the bottom of the whole matter once and for all.

CHAPTER 5

THE INTERVIEW

Gadsby started the interview by asking me to confirm my full name and cautioning me. He asked me if I understood the terms of the caution, and I confirmed that I did. He went on to explain:

> You have been asked to come to this police station because an allegation has been made … In essence, Mr Anqkar has alleged that in 1986, in October 1986, you arrested him, placed him in a van and assaulted him. That assault was beating, thumping, kicking and then culminated in you penetrating his anus, bottom, with an implement.

I was resolute in my reply. I told the detectives that I did not know a Mr Anqkar and had no memory of such an incident taking place – the allegation seemed totally malicious and false. I also explained that the police had provided me with very little information, and unless they were able to give me more details about what I was doing specifically in October 1986, there was little more I could do to help with their investigation.

Gadsby then asked me general questions about 1986. I confirmed that I was of police constable rank at the time and that I had joined the service in 1982. In October 1986, I was on the crime squad, working on a district out of Putney, south-west London.

He then asked again if I knew Harry Anqkar; I assume he was attempting to trigger a memory and further elaborated by describing him:

'Black lad, part of the Battersea gangs that perhaps the crime squad was targeting ... I don't know what they were called back there but you were given a selection of individuals to go out and look at.'

He had it wrong. I told him that the crime squad covered all sorts of crimes: burglary, robberies, handling stolen goods, drugs, and that we even worked with murder squads from time to time, too. He went back to asking me about the incident, wanting me again to confirm if I was sure I had no recollection of what happened. I replied:

'Well, beating a prisoner up, in the van, and forcing something ... that's total nonsense.'

Gadsby continued to probe. I continued to state that I had never physically or sexually assaulted anyone. Going on what little information the police had given me so far, I had apparently arrested Anqkar for carrying a knife, and given that I had nothing to hide, I admitted that it was possible that I'd been the arresting officer at the time. My arrest rate had been over 100 criminals a year; there was no way I could remember the name of everyone that I'd arrested in my thirty years of service.

We moved on to the type of van Anqkar had described in his statement. I believed we used Ford Transit vans at the time, but that if we were assigned to the crime squad and we arrested someone, we would take the person back to the station in the crime squad car. That was standard practice.

Failing to get anything out of me that would corroborate Anqkar's claims of being forced into a marked Sherpa, Gadsby tried a different tack. He questioned me about the use of handcuffs: was it usual practice to handcuff the suspect when arresting them? I responded that 'at that time in '86, it wasn't standard procedure to handcuff prisoners ... normally with juveniles and the elderly, or even females, you wouldn't. It's only people who were violent you would put handcuffs on. It wasn't a standard procedure at the time.'

Gadsby then tried to ask the same question in another way: if someone was carrying an offensive weapon, such as a knife, would the risk assessment be changed? I replied by saying that it depended on the prisoner, but handcuffs wouldn't always be necessary.

When doing undercover work, police officers would usually work in pairs and rarely carried any safety equipment, as this would single you out as an officer immediately. I told Gadsby this, after he tried to establish what sort of police safety equipment I was carrying at the time.

He then asked me if I remembered who I was paired up with while I was on the crime squad, and whether I had had any problems with the people I worked with. I remember thinking it was an odd question to ask, but I responded anyway. I told Gadsby that I remembered having a difficult time while in the crime squad; people would call me names, send racist messages and even my police uniform was destroyed. He then went on to ask me if I remembered who the perpetrators were and if I could provide names. I could not understand what this had to do with the alleged assault and I put this question to him. He replied: 'Mr Virdi, I'm asking the questions and I'm putting that question to you...'

I was growing frustrated and suspicious. Why was he asking me questions about my relationship with my colleagues? How was this related to Anqkar?

Plus, there was one more thing that stuck in my mind, which I put to Gadsby:

Well, the other thing that's very suspicious is, because you mentioned the name George. I would never ever use that with a prisoner. Because my name is Gurpal. So the only person who would have come out with this is a police officer. So if a police officer is trying to stitch me up with this...

I felt like I was on high alert. Something was going on, something much bigger than this alleged assault. Gadsby assured me that no other police officers were involved, and that the allegation was being made by Anqkar. He then went back to questioning me about the officers who victimised me while I was at Battersea. This was getting ridiculous. My solicitor intervened and questioned the relevance. Gadsby simply replied: 'It is relevant. And the reason will become apparent during the interview.'

Gadsby refused to give me any explanation as to why I was being asked about the racism I had faced when I worked in the crime squad, and how any of this was relevant to the alleged assault. Despite asking him repeatedly for more information, the officer flat out refused. I thought he was supposed to be open with me and I was trying to help him as much as I could, but I didn't feel he was doing the same for me.

Gadsby continued his questioning and asked if I had ever had any racist attitudes towards sections of the community. I told him that the black community welcomed me in south London, and that the local community were very supportive. His follow-up question returned again to naming the officers who had victimised me. I was not going to start naming names, so I asked him to consult the reports that I had filed with inspectors and sergeants at the time.

I was then asked if I had ever used the term 'nigger'. I answered that I had not. Gadsby was not getting the answers that he wanted from me, and I could see he was getting increasingly frustrated:

Harry, Mr Anqkar, and I'm not gonna go into depth on this 'cos you saying it didn't happen, but it's quite right and proper that I put his account to you, I mean there's not much more detail than basically is on the disclosure but he said that he was arrested in the Clapham Junction area. He

was handcuffed and put in the back of the van. You asked
him for his name and he said: 'What kind of name is that
for a nigger,' and slapped him hard in the face. Does that
bring back any memories?

I confirmed that I had never done that. I said it would not
have even been procedure at the time. When making an
arrest, you ask for a person's name while still on the street;
you do not wait until a van arrives, put the suspect into
the back and then ask their name. Gadsby replied that he
was simply repeating what Anqkar had told him. He asked
me again if I had slapped Anqkar and called him a nigger.
Once again, I told him that I hadn't. I made it clear that this was
not a case of me failing to remember an incident that allegedly happened twenty-eight years ago: I was saying 'no' because
I knew there was no way I would have ever behaved in such
a way.

Gadsby continued to recount Anqkar's story of how I had
thrown him around the van, kicking and punching him.
Enough was enough. I could think of only one way to get to
the bottom of the matter – I would need the arrest notes, and
my pocket book notes. I was safe in the knowledge that I had
not committed the assault.

Whenever someone is arrested and taken into the station,
a police officer has to complete paperwork – this includes
what was known back then as an Arrest Form 74. I wanted
Gadsby to show me Anqkar's arrest form, which would easily
prove whether I had been the arresting officer. As I knew the

allegations against me were false, I strongly suspected that my name would be absent from the arrest form and would therefore prove my innocence.

'Well you, hang on, you're presuming a lot of things here,' I said. 'You're only taking the word of an individual, whereas you've got police records, you've got custody records and you've got court records. And let's have them now and let's see what really did happen.'

Gadsby replied: 'Mmm, as I explained, from twenty-eight years ago, all paper records have been destroyed.'

I did not believe what he was saying for a second.

Gadsby went back to the assault: 'You sat on him and then placed what he says, what he thought was a truncheon or something similar into his bottom through his clothing and forced it up his bottom. Did that happen?'

I disagreed with the statement and told him that I wouldn't have been carrying a truncheon, especially if I was in plain clothes. Gadsby then backtracked and said that Anqkar believed it could have been an ASP that was forced up his bottom. I was confused: did Anqkar say it was a truncheon or an ASP? I told Gadsby that I was pretty certain the Metropolitan Police did not start using ASPs until the late 1980s/early 1990s.

DC GADSBY: 'I think you're right, I think it was later than that. But what's right and fair is what Mr Anqkar's saying. I'm telling you...'

G VIRDI: 'You know he's telling a lie then, isn't he?'

DC GADSBY: 'I don't know if it's a lie or if he's mistaken.'

Again, I was flabbergasted. Why on earth was I sitting here being interviewed when the investigating officer wasn't sure if Anqkar's story was true or false? And if Anqkar had been mistaken about an ASP being used, why hadn't his story been discussed and verified ahead of my interview?

We moved on to what happened after Anqkar was taken to the police station, following the alleged assault. Gadsby described how Anqkar claimed that he had been booked in, interviewed and then released. He then appeared in court a month later and was convicted for carrying an offensive weapon and for a public order matter. Gadsby asked if any of this new information had jogged my memory; did I now remember the incident? Of course, I didn't.

I referred back to the paperwork – I knew it still existed. If Anqkar had been convicted, there would have been a lot of paperwork detailing his crime and the conviction. This would include police records, incident report books, custody records and court records, to name a few.

The response I got was this: 'Yeah, Mr Virdi, I've said this four times now, all the records for 1986, with the exception of one court document … have all been destroyed. Documentation back then was destroyed after seven years, so there are no records.'

If Gadsby's claim was true, this meant that all documentation regarding any arrests carried out by the Met in 1986 would have been destroyed, which was deeply concerning.

I decided to ask Gadsby why Anqkar hadn't made the allegation at the time, and he replied by telling me he was not
at liberty to comment. His response infuriated me; surely
an important part of the investigation would have been to
find out why Anqkar was only coming forward now, twenty-
eight years after the alleged assault. I challenged Gadsby on
this point and asked whether he was leading the investigation or if it was one of his superiors. He said a more senior
officer was in charge.

It was at this point that Gadsby explained why my relationship with my colleagues in 1986 was relevant. This is
when the interview took a turn for the worst. It was also at
this stage in the interview that it became clear this was no
longer solely an allegation by a man named Anqkar. The
Metropolitan Police was also involved:

You were working with Tom Makins that day … Tom
Makins did leave the MPS, Metropolitan Police Service, and
went to Guernsey where he retired fairly recently … He remembers that incident quite well, very well in fact. He was
tape-recorded interviewed in Guernsey several months ago
and he's provided a statement. So yes, there aren't any paper
records, IRBs [incident report books] or Custody Records;
however, there is evidence from an individual and serving
officer at the time. He remembers the stop, he thought
Anqkar was arrested for theft, didn't remember anything
about a knife. He remembers being in the back of the van;
he was there, you were there, Anqkar was there.

He said that a scuffle started and you started punching and kicking Mr Anqkar. He was a fifteen-year-old boy, quite small, quite short. He considers that the force you used was totally unnecessary and totally unreasonable. He did not see any sexual assault, he didn't see you putting anything up Mr Anqkar's bottom or anus, but clearly remember you punching and kicking him and holding him down. And he felt that this was totally unnecessary. He shouted at you several times for you to stop and tried to pull you off, but you continued in your assault. Do you have anything to say about Mr Makins's account, Mr Virdi?

I had no words. I was speechless. My heart sank. I vaguely remembered Makins as he had also been part of the crime squad. From what I could recall, he was only with the squad for a short period of time, so I barely knew him and I had no idea what would have motivated him to make this statement. I told Gadsby that Makins's statement was false.

I was frustrated. The disclosure provided before the interview did not mention Tom Makins; it stated clearly that there was no passenger in the passenger seat:

GV: 'OK. What, you're gonna start introducing evidence without disclosure are you?'
DCG: 'As you know, an interviewing officer can produce whatever evidence he or she wants in an interview. Not obliged to produce any or disclose any evidence.'

You would think that an investigating officer would want to provide me with as much information as possible, given that this alleged assault took place twenty-eight years ago. Gadsby was doing nothing to help me; in fact, it seemed that his interviewing tactic was to intermittently disclose new information in what I assume was an attempt to try to catch me out, so that I would unwittingly corroborate Anqkar's and Makins's stories.

I was keen to learn more about Makins's story, in particular what he did and did not see. His testimony was unconvincing and I could already spot holes in it.

GV: 'Makins… so he's confirmed that the assault did not take place?'
DCG: 'No, he's confirmed the assault did take place.'
GV: 'No, the, the indecent assault didn't take place.'
DCG: 'He can't comment on that. He didn't see the indecent assault.'
DN: 'Is he saying it's possible? Because it beggars belief that he wouldn't see something like that.'
DCG: 'He's saying that he didn't see it, he's saying it was dark in the van but he didn't see it or he didn't hear anything to lead him to believe something like that happened.'
DN: 'Well, I think we can take it as it didn't happen then.'
DCG: 'I don't think you can take it by that at all.'
GV: 'As a, as a police officer he should have made a complaint then, shouldn't he?'
DN: 'It, it does, it all but, all but confirms it. I mean it

would beggar belief that he just wouldn't see that, even in a darkened van.'

As my solicitor and I were grappling with Makins's evidence, Gadsby suggested that instead of making judgements on what we did or didn't think, we simply needed to look at the evidence 'as it sits at the moment'. Gadsby asked whether, after hearing Makins's testimony, I had changed my views on what had happened in 1986. I told him I hadn't. He wanted to know whether I had been racist towards Anqkar; I confirmed that I hadn't.

Gadsby then added another police officer to the mix: Danny Dwyer.

'Do you remember an incident in Clapham Junction some time in 2000, not 2000, sorry, 1986, possibly 1987, where a black man walked past you and spat and you held him hard up against a shutter of a shop, and again you were pulled off by an officer?'

My solicitor had to step in again at this point.

'I don't think it's appropriate for you to start answering questions about allegations not disclosed to us and for which you are not here as a volunteer to be interviewed.'

She advised me not to answer any questions that had no relevance to Anqkar's allegations.

Gadsby told us again that his questions were relevant to the allegations against me. He wanted me to confirm that I had never exhibited racist behaviour. When faced with these wild accusations I responded: 'I, I totally disagree because the amount of work I have done with the African–Caribbean community and the BPA, Black Police Association; it's all recorded.'

After a long pause, Gadsby said the following:

Now that you've heard what Mr Makins has had to say, I think you said when I was referring to his statement that 'it's untrue, it's untrue.' Why do you have any reason to believe why he would provide a signed MG11 [a witness statement] saying that happened if it didn't happen? Obviously you can't guess, but do you have any knowledge for why he would provide the statement? Clearly, potentially committing perjury if this went to court, certainly committing offences under the magistrates act, and he would know that being a senior police officer?

If this case went to court, Tom Makins would be giving evidence that was incorrect. I had no idea why Tom would say such things, as I barely knew him. I had developed many enemies in the police force over the years, but anything I thought or said about Tom would have been speculation. I was stunned.

The line of questioning then turned to self-defence: was there any chance I could have committed this offence if I had been acting in self-defence? The answer was no. Self-defence does not result in indecently assaulting a minor in the back of a van.

Gadsby had clearly decided I was guilty; I needed real,

tangible evidence to prove my innocence. So I went back to asking about the paperwork; after all, I knew it still existed. While I was a police officer, I had always ensured that I did everything by the book, so I knew that, back then, every time anyone made an arrest the following paperwork would have to be completed:

- Incident report book – in this notebook an officer would record brief notes on the arrest. This would include notes on the circumstances of the arrest and witnesses involved.
- Custody records – when at the police station, a custody record would be completed, naming the arresting officer and the witnessing officer amongst other details.
- Full set of notes – while the prisoner is in custody, a full report would be logged on the arrest and next steps e.g. charges and court date to be set.
- Phone call to Scotland Yard – if the arrest concerned a juvenile, a phone call to Scotland Yard would always be made to record the incident.
- Phone call to an appropriate adult.
- Fingerprints and photographs – always taken from a juvenile.

Earlier in the interview, Gadsby had said that all documents had been destroyed. And, fair enough, it was possible that the case file had been destroyed after seven years. However, fingerprints, photographs and the Arrest Form 74 are never destroyed. A copy of the arrest form is scanned immediately into the Police National Computer (PNC), and this has always been the case, even back in 1986.

Think about it this way: if you wanted to employ a nanny to look after your child, you would want to know if that person had been arrested for carrying a knife twenty-eight years ago. In order to obtain this information, you would ask your potential nanny to show you their enhanced CRB check. An enhanced CRB check would detail any time the potential nanny had been arrested or convicted throughout their life. Where do you think people carrying out enhanced CRB checks get their data from? The Police National Com puter. So, if Anqkar and Makins were telling the truth, details of his arrest in 1986 would have been recorded on the PNC. And if they were telling the truth, my name would come up as the arresting officer.

Gadsby's response when I asked again for the paperwork:

DCG: 'You won't have, there isn't any paperwork. Fifth time I said that.'
GV: 'If Mr Makins was seeing this force, why did he not report it to a senior officer?'
DCG: 'He didn't.'
GV: 'Well, there you go … amazing, you find Mr Virdi to find an allegation on and nobody else.'

I asked Gadsby what the next steps would be. He confirmed that the case file would be sent to the Crown Prosecution Service (CPS). This organisation is the principal prosecuting authority for England and Wales – it acts independently of the Metropolitan Police and makes the final decision on whether or not cases should be prosecuted. It also determines the appropriate charges, advising the police during the early stages of investigations, and prepares cases and presents them at court. My experience with the CPS had not been good – I was not hopeful.

I said my goodbyes to Ms Naaman and thanked her for her time; she confirmed that she would write to me, confirming that her firm would take my case on.

I left the interview with Gadsby in shock. Most of all, I felt betrayed by the Metropolitan Police and my former colleagues whom I had worked with all those years ago – why would Makins and Dwyer make statements against me? I couldn't figure it out and it was extremely disturbing.

I needed to take action and I needed a plan. There was no way I was letting the Metropolitan Police destroy everything I had worked so hard for, on the basis of a false allegation. Most of all, I had to defend my honour.

CHAPTER 6

MURKY WATERS

The bus ride home was a blur. My mind filled with questions from the interview. Who was this Anqkar character and was he trying to make false allegations against me? I was in a state of complete shock; I felt betrayed by the service I had given thirty years of my life to, and by the colleagues I had worked closely alongside.

As I opened the front door, I took a deep breath and was greeted by a worried Sathat. She was the only one home as both the kids were at work.

'I'm being stitched up again,' I told her, trying to make light of the horrendous situation. It didn't get a laugh. I explained what had happened, the extent of the allegations and the further disclosures that I had been provided with. She was in total shock, as was I.

Over lunch, we drew parallels between the new allegations and those made in 1998, during the first case. It was slowly dawning on us that perhaps history was about to repeat itself. However, in an attempt to reassure Sathat (and myself), I explained that if this case was anything like the last one, the CPS would definitely throw it out as there was a serious lack of evidence. A historical allegation, one inconsistent witness, no documents and no concrete facts were not sufficient cause for the CPS to proceed with the case. With this in mind, we decided our course of action at this point was just to tell the children, our close family and friends.

The first person I contacted was Sir Peter Bottomley, a Conservative MP who had provided such great support during my first case, and whom I was sure would assist me again. I wrote him a short email, requesting a meeting with him as soon as possible. He responded swiftly, asking me to contact his office the next day.

My next task was to make a Freedom of Information (FoI) request to the Met regarding historical allegations. I wanted to know how many Met officers had been interviewed for offences that took place over twenty-five years ago. I also wanted a breakdown of these interviews by ethnicity. The Met later informed me that from 1994 to 2014, fifteen officers were investigated, of whom only one was an Asian officer: me.

● ● ●

Jasbir Johal, 'JJ', is an ethnic minority Met officer who retired after serving twenty-nine years, a colleague and a very good friend of mine. After joining the police in 1980, Jasbir was posted to south London while I worked in nearby Battersea. I knew that Jasbir was very familiar with Battersea, so I thought that he might be able to remember something that would help my case. Originally from Nottingham, Jasbir decided to apply for the Metropolitan Police after he and his wife were married and the couple settled in London.

I always made a point of introducing myself to ethnic minority officers and police staff. There weren't many of us there at the time, so it was always reassuring in case someone needed help during difficult times. After I moved from Battersea, Jasbir was promoted to sergeant in the Hillingdon division, before becoming an inspector and joining a specialist squad at New Scotland Yard. He spent a few years as a detective inspector in Enfield but, unfortunately, was taken ill and forced to go on restricted duties before eventually taking early retirement.

Although I wanted to contact Jasbir, I was hesitant. Healthwise, he wasn't doing too well, so I didn't want to burden him with my latest problems with the Met. But I needed information, reassurance and guidance from my friend so, despite my reservations, I called him and arranged to meet him at his home later that afternoon.

'So what's this all about?' Jasbir asked. I felt a surge of anger and dread rise through me as I had to explain the awful situation.

'Clearly they're out to prosecute you and it would appear that they haven't learnt any lessons from the past,' was Jasbir's initial reaction.

I asked him if he remembered any of the characters involved. He couldn't place Anqkar, but recalled Makins moving to Guernsey and Danny Dwyer's having behaved controversially.

'What was Anqkar arrested for?' Jasbir asked.

'For possession of an offensive weapon. I've arrested so many people; I don't remember that name. In fact, I am the one who used to intervene when black people used to get beaten up.'

'Did they show you your arrest notes, documents, court records?'

'No, I kept asking for them but they claimed everything had been destroyed.'

From what he had heard so far, Jasbir thought that this looked like a stitch-up. It was far too convenient that all the paperwork that could prove my innocence had been destroyed. The only saving grace was the PNC records. I was sure that they were out there, and if and when they were made available to me, I would be able to prove my innocence and refute the lies that had been told. Jasbir agreed that there was no way the PNC documents would have been destroyed (regardless of what Gadsby had claimed in the interview). He was also certain that court convictions papers, custody documents and stop and search records for Anqkar would be available.

Another thing to address was collapsible truncheons. We both assured each other that we weren't given truncheons at Battersea. Jasbir confirmed that he was given his while serving in Hayes in the 1990s and I'm confident that I didn't receive mine until I was in Ealing in the mid-'90s. We had been issued collapsible truncheons and CS gas canisters at the same time, so the date had stuck in our heads, and it certainly wasn't when we had been in south London together.

Talking things over with Jasbir was reassuring and helped to ease my nerves. As he was aware of what happened with my last case and the implications it had on senior officers and their careers, he understood why the Met was targeting me again.

Jasbir went on to explain:

You know, after the racist hate mail case, there were a lot of senior officers who were very unhappy with the decision made by the employment tribunal. They wanted you out because the truth was hard to swallow and their careers were halted as they were labelled racists, yet again. They've been out to get you and, although it's an abuse of power, they can do so. They just want to show to the public that you're a criminal.

'I've done nothing wrong,' I responded. 'I just want them to leave me and my family alone. I left in 2012 so that I could move on. Like yours, my children are adults now and I know that this is going to be difficult. When this is over, I will need to leave the country. If I don't, they won't leave me alone.'

'They'll drag it along then drop it. Don't worry. Look at how many cases they have dropped against white officers because of delay. Your allegations go back what, twenty-eight years without any documents? Everything will be fine.'

I wished I had his confidence. I was conscious of having taken up a lot of his time, so I thanked him and headed home.

The next thing to do was to tell the children. They had

been dragged through the same murky waters in the late '90s, and now that they were adults they had a right to know the details. After all, it would be better for my kids to hear about the allegations from me than from some other source. I also had to consider the effect of the news on Sathat's elderly parents, who were not in the best of health. I had sadly lost both of my own parents during the last case – they had died before seeing my name cleared. I sincerely hoped that history would not repeat itself.

Dinner was filled with the usual chit-chat and the hum of the television in the background. I could see Sathat was not herself and, I suppose, nor was I. As we came to the end of our meal, I broke the news to the kids. They were shocked and alarmed; it was heartbreaking to see. We would have to go through the same trauma again. Kesar, my daughter, was the first to speak.

'When did this happen?' she asked.

'Well, I went to the police station today to be interviewed, but a couple of police officers came to the house a few days ago.'

'Do you remember this guy? Did anything happen?'

'No – I don't recall him at all. The allegation he has made is totally false.'

I could see the look of great concern spread across her face. 'This sounds serious. What are the consequences, should the CPS decide to proceed with the case?' We all looked at one another, not wanting to acknowledge what the actual consequences would be.

I had to stay positive, if not for my own sake then at the very least for the sake of my family, so I simply replied: 'Let's just take it one step at a time. Hopefully this will all be sorted out and nothing will come of it.'

After a pause, my son, Kushal, spoke up. He asked me a simple question that brought tears to Sathat's eyes: 'Why do the police keep harassing you, Dad?'

I answered as honestly as I could: 'This is the price you have to pay for being an honest officer and for fighting inequality.'

More silence. Finally, Kesar spoke up: 'We'll get through this together.'

• • •

Sathat is a very tidy and organised person and for years she has accused me of being a hoarder. She's nagged me endlessly for keeping documents that are several years old and which take up a lot of space in the house. But I was sure, given the allegations levelled against me, that this was the one time she was grateful that I was such a hoarder.

After dinner, my detective hat was back on. I decided to sift through my documents dating back to my time at Battersea. Commendations, appraisals, transfer applications, newspaper cuttings – anything that could shed light on the allegations against me. The alleged incident had occurred nearly thirty years ago and my memory wasn't quite what it used to be, so I was hoping to find something that would jog it – anything that could plausibly help.

CHAPTER 7

INNOCENT UNTIL PROVEN GUILTY?

Given the serious nature and potential implications of the allegation, the following day I decided it was time to tell more people what was happening. The first person I approached was Rob Wyatt at the Youth Justice Panel. Considering that my job as part of the panel involved working with young people, it was only right that I informed Rob of the allegations levelled against me straight away.

'I wouldn't worry about it, Gurpal. I am not concerned. I believe you didn't do it. The offence is far too old anyway and will probably not result in charges of prosecution,' Rob said reassuringly.

'Do you want me to carry on with the panel or do you want me to step down?' I asked.

'Let's wait to see what happens.'

I was grateful for his understanding and the faith he had shown in me, but, personally, I believed that the best thing to do would be for me to step down. Any negative publicity could have been extremely damaging and I didn't want it to affect anyone.

• • •

These days you can learn so much from the internet. Really, the vast amount of information available at your fingertips is incredible. A life before the world wide web is really quite unimaginable now, so I decided the best place to start my investigation would be Google. What I wanted to find out was who exactly Anqkar was and what Tom Makins and Danny Dwyer were up to these days. Were the two men who had fanned the flames still active officers or had they retired? Had either man been involved in anything like this before? Unfortunately, what I had found was very limited. Dwyer had retired from the force but was now an instructor at a police training school. As for Makins, I could find very little information about him online and Anqkar was a complete dead end.

A couple of days later, I was scheduled to work a morning shift at Linkline. As soon as I got into work, I explained what had happened to my line manager. Again, I was reassured that they knew I was innocent and that these were historical allegations so I should try not to worry. Everyone I spoke to about the case was in agreement: they all believed I would never do such a thing. The general consensus was that, given how long ago the alleged incident had taken place, surely the case would not make it to court. Words of reassurance from friends were important to me: to have the support of the people around me, those who knew me best, was wonderful.

My manager said that I could continue working on

scheduled shifts, but that a conversation was needed after the CPS decided whether or not they wanted to proceed with the case. That night, I decided to email Sadiq Khan MP, my Labour Party mentor, hoping to seek advice in finding a way forward. Imogen Cahill, Sadiq Khan's parliamentary apprentice, responded with a provisional date to meet at Portcullis House on 30 April at 11 a.m.

• • •

On Monday 31 March 2014, I made my way to Westminster for my morning meeting with Sir Peter Bottomley. He went through the two pages of disclosure and asked me about the allegations and we discussed my recent police interview, while Sir Peter took notes on his notepad. After going through the specifics, he reached for his phone and dialled the number for Balham Juvenile Court. There was a possibility that Anqkar's records could be tracked down, particularly if he had been a young offender and known to youth services. Sir Peter wanted to know what had happened since the last accusations and my retirement. I held nothing back as I trusted him 100 per cent.

We spent two hours discussing the allegations and Peter assured me that he would contact DPS to express his concerns regarding the situation. Speaking to Peter eased my worries slightly – he is a well-respected MP and our conversation gave me a renewed sense of optimism, knowing that he would be fighting my corner.

Until I knew what was going to happen next, there was little I could do apart from get on with life as usual. I honestly believed that the CPS would drop the case, but I still felt like a victim of the Met, so I wrote to the Home Affairs Select Committee, asking them to look into my case of continued harassment.

The last case had taken its toll on my health: it had caused me to develop high blood pressure and left me suffering from post-traumatic stress disorder. With my well-being in mind, I thought it was best to book an appointment with the GP for a check-up. After all, if I was going to go head to head with the Met, I would need my strength.

My GP, Dr Patel, could tell that something was up as soon as I walked into his office. He has been my family doctor for over thirty years, having also looked after both my parents. I had gone to see him several times during my first case and he knew all about the details.

'What's wrong? Has something happened at home?'

'Not exactly… The Met Police are after me again.'

I told Dr Patel about what had happened and the toll it was taking on my health, the pressure it had put on me and my concerns about my blood pressure. I found that telling my story didn't get any easier. Putting into words what the Met was trying to do to me and my family was painful and saddening.

'Why do they keep harassing you?'

This was often the response I was met with when I explained what had happened. I wished I had a simple answer for such a simple question.

'I don't know why.'

'Look, I wouldn't worry yourself. If the guy was telling the truth, he would have come forward many years ago. I suspect there is something else going on though – it feels like the Met are up to something.'

Too right, they were. And even Dr Patel could see that.

15 APRIL

For the past sixteen years, 15 April has always conjured up bad memories and feelings of distress: it was the day the Met raided our family home in 1998. I'm not the kind of man to hold a grudge, but I'm still working on moving on from that incident. Whenever I think back to that day, the sense of utter betrayal still comes flooding back and I'm not sure it will ever go away.

It was around mid-afternoon on 15 April 2014 when I received a phone call from my solicitor, Ms Naaman, saying she had some news. My stomach tightened.

'The Met Police have passed this on to the CPS.'

'Any idea when they'll make a decision?'

'Nothing yet. Once I get more details, I will contact you.'

She went on to say: 'DC Gadsby also raised another issue with me. When he served you with the letter inviting you to attend an interview, he stated that you mentioned that you work with children. Given the nature of one of the allegations, sexual assault, he has asked if you would clarify this.'

I didn't clarify anything for DC Gadsby. I knew that if I gave the police any information they would only use it against me and try to discredit me.

Later that day, I received an email from Ms Naaman, informing me that I would have to attend Hounslow police station, but she would, unfortunately, not be accompanying me. This was highly unusual behaviour and immediately got my guard up. It happened so suddenly, but I found myself left without any legal representation.

Later in the day, I received another email from the same law firm notifying me that another solicitor would be taking over the case. I was unimpressed.

25 APRIL

On the morning of 25 April, I made my way to Hounslow police station to receive the CPS's verdict. Why they wanted to see me in person was perplexing – and a police station was really the last place I wanted to be. As I arrived at the station, I could feel a knot starting to form in my stomach and I felt increasingly uneasy. Two police officers – Detective Inspector Francis De Juan and Detective Sergeant Joanne Johnson – invited me into a small, dark office. There was no small talk; they simply handed me the two summonses that had been issued by the courts, detailing my court date and the offences I was being charged with. How could accusations that were entirely false be going ahead?

A summons is normally sent via the post, so it was unsettling that I had been asked to pick mine up in person. Something did not sit right.

'Is there anything you wish to say, Mr Virdi?' the police officers asked.

'No.'

'I also have here a press release,' DI De Juan said, while handing over a third document. 'This has already been released to the media, but this is a copy for you.'

FOR OFFER: Former MPS officer, Gurpal Virdi (DOB 07/09/58) of Hounslow, has been summoned to appear on 30/05/14 before Westminster Magistrates Court to answer to:

Offence: Between 30/09/1986 and 31/12/1986 within the jurisdiction of the Central Criminal Court, Mr Gurpal Virdi, being a Public Officer, namely a Metropolitan Police officer, and acting as such, without reasonable excuses or justification, wilfully misconducted himself to such a degree as to amount to an abuse of the public's trust in that office.

Contrary to Common Law.

Offence: Indecent assault on a boy under the age of sixteen years (Section fifteen of the Sexual Offences Act 1956)

Particulars: Between 30/09/1986 and 31/12/1986 within the jurisdiction of the CCC you indecently assaulted a boy under sixteen.

The summons follows an investigation by the

Directorate of Professional Standards into an allegation of
an historic indecent assault.

Is this why they wanted to give me my summons in person?
To give me a copy of a press release that not only revealed my
personal details but also completely discredited me? I was
both without legal representation or an independent witness.
I was left completely vulnerable and alone.

'So this is what this is all about then – me coming to the
station just so you can give me this press release?'

The officers looked me straight in the eye and simply
smiled.

'What has happened to the allegations I made – police
officers perverting the court of justice and making false statements? Have they been recorded; will anything happen?' I
asked.

'What allegations?'

'The ones I made during my interview with Gadsby.'

'I don't know anything about those, Mr Virdi. However, I
will mention it to the officer investigating the case, who will
contact you to discuss these further.'

I left the police station traumatised. Why were they
doing this to me? Why was I already being treated as
guilty? The press release I had been handed didn't specify
that the alleged incident had taken place in October 1986,
instead the Met was claiming it had occurred between 30
September and 31 December 1986. What on earth were they
playing at?

As soon as I got home, I went straight to my study, as I needed to know how far the news had spread. The alleged assault was already doing the rounds and a quick Google search showed that BBC London News and local media, such as the *Hounslow Chronicle*, were already reporting on the press release that I'd only just received. Clearly the press release had been given to the media with an embargo till 11 a.m.

The headlines were damning and straight to the point. BBC London News ran with: 'Retired officer accused of indecent assault of boy, 16'. The report continued: 'A former Met police officer has been summoned to appear in court to face a charge of indecently assaulting a boy under sixteen while he was in police custody, Scotland Yard has said.'

I felt sick to my stomach. The headlines were nothing more than character assassinations; their sole purpose was not to inform but to condemn me as guilty. In my opinion and experience, the Met will use this strategy to vilify their suspects and encourage the public to skim over the facts. The timing was convenient for the Met – the local elections were just around the corner and no doubt such headlines would sabotage my election prospects. I had to contact my Labour Party representative to inform him of the summons and request a meeting. Even after my past experiences with the Met, I guess I still had some faith in the British criminal system. I still believed justice would prevail and that one was 'innocent until proven guilty' – I was obviously too naive.

Peter was the next person I contacted; I desperately needed advice from a trusted friend. Midway through firing off an email to Peter, Sathat entered the study. She was, of course, anxious to know what had happened at the police station, so I handed her the summons and the press release. The news silenced her. She stood shocked and motionless. I tried to speak to her, but could see that nothing I was saying was getting through. She turned on her heels and walked out of the room. It was a lot to process, that much was obvious, so I followed her and sat her down.

'How are you feeling?' I could see that her breathing was ragged and she was starting to turn a pale yellow colour. She put a hand to her chest.

'My heart's pounding. I feel dizzy. I feel like I can't breathe,' she said faintly.

'Take deep breaths,' I instructed her. Sathat has always been a healthy woman. She takes good care of herself and I've never known her to suffer from any major illnesses. The sight of her struggling to breathe panicked me – I had never seen her like this. Immediately, I called our GP to try to schedule an emergency appointment, but he wasn't available so I drove Sathat to the urgent care centre at West Middlesex Hospital.

As soon as we arrived, a nurse carried out preliminary checks on Sathat, before she ushered Sathat into a consultation room. I waited outside; the wait was agonising and I had never felt so helpless. It turned out Sathat's blood pressure was sky high. It pained me that my cool, calm and collected wife was suffering in this way. She was prescribed medication immediately – never a good sign. From my own experience with high blood pressure, I knew that doctors would initially advise patients to make changes to their lifestyle and diet and would only prescribe medication if the changes were ineffective. So for Sathat to have been prescribed medication after her first consultation must have meant that she was in a bad way. Sathat had always been my rock; she had helped me overcome so many obstacles and I knew that it was a selfish thought, but I couldn't help but think that I really needed her strength.

When we got home, Kushal was already in. His friends had seen the news on TV.

'Dad, some friends said they saw the case mentioned on TV; what's going on?'

It was strange to know that he had heard the news before we had been able to break it to him: TV, the internet and social media are marvellous yet horrifying inventions. I knew that I had to be honest with Kushal – there was no point sugar-coating things – so I showed him the summons and the press release. He was silenced by the news.

I called Kesar and asked her to come home early. She has always been very close to her mum and I knew that Sathat would find solace in her daughter's presence. I decided against breaking the news over text – I didn't feel it was the kind of thing you could really share via a message. Kesar has always been the more logical of our children, so the first thing she asked was: 'What's going to happen now? What's our next step? Who are we going to contact?

The news had ruined our appetites, but I knew it was no use not eating, so I made us dinner. I wanted to protect my family from what was happening; I felt that it was my responsibility to shield them from the evil in the world, but the situation was completely out of my hands.

After a sleepless night, I decided that I had to do something about the situation. I needed to try to regain some control. After an early morning phone call informing me that my solicitor had been changed for a third time, I knew my number-one priority was to find a new legal team. One that had no connections or bias towards the Metropolitan Police – a team that was strong, independent and reliable. There was too much at stake to risk using a biased representative.

As I was racking my brain for the names of potential firms I could turn to, I remembered Harriet Wistrich of Birnberg Peirce & Partners. We had met when her firm was working on another high-profile case. A human rights lawyer, Harriet specialised in cases holding the police and other state bodies to account for abuses of power. Perhaps it seems strange that I chose a human rights lawyer, but these false allegations were an infringement of my rights. I did not deserve the continued harassment from the Met; I too had a right to a happy family life. With this in mind, I sent Harriet the paperwork I had accumulated: the letter from the Met inviting me to the station, the disclosure, the summons document and the press release.

I received a call from Alan Olive, a Labour Party representative based in the London regional office who was following up the email I had sent to my Labour representative.

I knew Alan already; he had been very supportive of my desire to become a local councillor and of my pledge to 'clean up' Hounslow, which included eradicating bad practices, introducing fresh candidates into the election process and reopening the Cranford ward with the proper selection processes in place.

'Hello, Gurpal, this is Alan.' I thanked him for getting in touch. 'I have read about the allegations in the local media. Do you want to discuss what's going on?'

'Yeah, fine. Well, as you know, an allegation of assault has been made against me, dating back to 1986. I haven't yet received full disclosure from the police; I was only provided very little information during my interview. Other than that, I don't know what to say – I presume that this is happening to me because of the history that I have with the police. In my opinion, Alan, it is probably just another attempt by the Met Police to discredit me.'

'Are you saying that it is a fit-up, Gurpal?'

'Alan, I have never withheld any information from the Labour Party about myself or the past. And most of what has happened to me in the past is in the public domain. So, yes, I would say it's a fit-up.'

'Right, in that case I will speak to the Labour Party lawyers and let them make a decision based on the information we have. I have to ask, Gurpal, is there any truth in the allegations?'

Alan had to ask that question, I understood that. It was a painful but fair question.

'No, Alan, there isn't. And it is fine for you to pass the matter on to the lawyers. I have no problems with that.'

Later that evening, I received another phone call. It was Alan.

'Gurpal, it's Alan again. Unfortunately, I have been told by the Labour Party lawyers that we will need to suspend you. There's too much pressure coming from the media and the hierarchy.'

'Who's putting the pressure on you?'

'The national press has been in touch.'

'Who else?'

'Locals from Hounslow, councillors, party officials.'

'Right, so much for innocent until proven guilty. Will you be putting this in writing then?'

'Yes, the compliance unit will be writing to you.'

'What will happen to my election campaign?'

'The Labour Party will no longer be supporting you as their candidate, so I'll leave it up to you to decide how you wish to proceed with your campaign.' And then he hung up.

It felt like I was in a boxing ring: only my hands were tied behind my back and I couldn't dodge the punches. It seemed to me that this was exactly what the Met wanted: to smear my campaign, to prevent me from getting elected in another public office, and it was all panning out exactly as they had hoped. But I hadn't done anything wrong! I felt utterly helpless.

There was a Labour Party campaign event later that evening, which I had been due to attend, but, shortly after the phone call from Alan, I received a call from another Labour official telling me that I was suspended from the party and would no longer be able to attend any functions. Word had spread and it seemed that Labour had washed their hands of me.

Phone calls from concerned friends and family, who wanted to make sure I was OK, flooded in. I appreciated everyone's support but I wasn't in the right frame of mind to go over what had happened repeatedly. Besides, how could I explain what was happening when I didn't fully understand myself? The whole thing was madness!

Reluctantly, I logged onto my laptop and did the one thing you're not supposed to do in this sort of situation: I Googled myself. Within seconds, I was faced with a number of headlines:

Retired officer accused of indecent assault of boy under 16

Ex-police officer accused of indecently assaulting boy

Former detective from Hounslow to appear in court over historic assault complaint

Former officer summonsed for indecent assault on boy

Ex-Met policeman accused of indecent assault on boy

Former Met PC arrested over indecent assault of boy

I don't like to wallow in self-pity, so I tried to do something productive at every given opportunity. I decided to email my local MP, Seema Malhotra, to request a meeting. I also gave her a brief outline of my history with the Met and the case so far. I hoped that she would intervene and bring the matter to the attention of the House of Commons.

Sadly, when I look back on those days, all I can remember is the number of people who turned their backs on me. They decided I was guilty so they cut off all contact. It was unsurprising, as the same thing had happened when I'd been accused of sending abusive and racist messages. In a way, it was enlightening, because it showed who my true friends were.

My suspension from the Labour Party was followed by a call from Sadiq Khan's office – they were cancelling my meeting. I asked for it to be rescheduled but my request was declined. Sadiq was supposed to be my mentor and I had thought he would support me in my time of need, but again his behaviour was unsurprising.

I received another blow when a letter from the Labour Party's compliance unit arrived in the post. It was a follow-up to my call with Alan, giving me a notice of administrative suspension from holding office or representing the Labour Party. This meant that I was banned from attending party meetings and could no longer be considered for selection as a Labour Party candidate. I had been officially ostracised by the party.

But it was not only Labour who turned their back on me. A number of staff associations have been set up within the Met to promote and look after the interests of ethnic minority officers. Over the years, I'd developed professional relationships with retired police officers who held prominent positions within these associations. These were influential officers and I had hoped that they would be able to help me during this difficult time. But, upon hearing the nature of the allegations, they would all come up with a polite excuse as to why they were unable to help. To rub salt in the wound, these were officers who had also faced various forms of discrimination and I had always given them my support. They were nowhere to be seen when I needed them.

After the news spread, I received an urgent meeting request from the senior management team at Linkline. Although I responded immediately, I never heard back from Linkline and they stopped asking me to take on shifts. I was being shut out.

It wasn't before long that I received a letter from Rob Wyatt, a youth offending officer from the Youth Justice Panel. The letter read: 'In discussing your current situation with the YOS Head of Services … it would not be appropriate for you to undertake any panel meetings until these proceedings have reached their conclusion.'

I had become a leper. None of my colleagues wanted to be associated with me. I was becoming more and more isolated and it was evident that a guilty verdict had already been decided.

Despite this, my family's support was resolute. Often we would discuss what to do next, and we came to the conclusion that the best thing for me to do would be to stand as an independent candidate during the local elections. Some of my so-called friends had abandoned me, but I still had plenty of support from neighbours and relatives. There were people in the Labour Party who objected to my suspension. One such person was Hardeep Sahota, Lord Indarjit Singh's press officer. I had met Hardeep through functions and my work with the police Sikh association, to which Lord Singh had been a contributor. When Hardeep heard the news, he called to express his support and explained that Lord Singh had been concerned about the allegations and was keen to do something to help.

Knowing that I had people behind me who supported me encouraged me to go ahead with the election. It felt like a way of retaliating; the Met had wanted me to fail and I was not going to go down without a fight.

CHAPTER 8

COUNCILLOR GURPAL VIRDI

I couldn't waste time on those who had abandoned me. Harriet, whom I had contacted regarding legal support, had provided me with the contact details for Matt Foot, a solicitor at her firm who was willing to take the case.

On Thursday 1 May 2014, I went to meet Matt at his office in Camden to discuss the allegations. I was filled with a mix of apprehension and anticipation. Would Matt Foot be the one? Would he lead the strong legal team I need? Would he work diligently to clear my name? Would he be up for a fight against the establishment? I went into the reception area; files lay everywhere and a large photocopier was pumping out photo-copies. Matt came to greet me and I immediately took a liking to him. I have always liked to think that I'm a good judge of character. Generally, my gut instinct proves correct. But I was still slightly cautious as the situation with my colleagues had taught me that sometimes I get it completely wrong.

'I remember you from my father's memorial service,' Matt told me.

His father, Paul Foot, had been a distinguished investigative journalist who had worked for *Private Eye*. Paul had followed my case in 1998 and had regularly written articles about it for the magazine. He had been a source of great support and continued to cover my case after I was cleared by the employment tribunal.

Three months after Paul's death, there had been a memorial service in his honour at the Hackney Empire in London. I had been asked to address the service by giving a talk on how much time Paul had spent writing about my case in the last few years of his life. I was delighted and honoured, but it proved a very nervous night, as I had never spoken in front of so many people with the stage lights focused on me.

Matt took me to his office, a small room with one window. There were files everywhere: some neatly stacked against a wall, while others were scattered on the floor. I couldn't help but chuckle, it made me think of Sathat complaining about my paperwork littered across the house – she would have gone mad if she'd seen this place. I started to tell Matt what had happened and showed him the two pages of disclosure – one being the letter and the other one that I was given before the interview – as well as the summons and press release.

'This is all you were given?' he asked.

'Yes, that is it.'

I could tell he was surprised with the limited paperwork I had been given. He started to ask about my history with the Met, my family and financial circumstances.

'You're not going to be eligible for legal aid, but we have to go through the motions for them to reject you.'

'That's fine, I will pay. How much do you think it will be?'

'It is not going to be cheap. And it will also depend on the preparatory work, barrister fees and court applications.'

I was very aware of the financial costs of trying to prove my innocence. But my honour and credibility were the most important things to me, and I was willing to take the financial hit. This was something that had to be done.

'I will ask the Police Federation for financial support but I can tell you now, they'll reject your firm,' I said. 'The federation refused to fund my employment tribunal case back in 2000.'

'Why is that?'

'Because the federation tends to encourage ex and current officers to use one of their recommended legal firms. It's rare for an officer to look for their own legal representation and I don't think the Met likes it when officers do, as it means that the chosen lawyer will be out of the Met's circle of influence and will have its client's, and not the Met's, best interests at heart.'

Matt paused for a moment before responding: 'I suspected that might be the case. Right, the first thing is to prepare for the hearing at Westminster Magistrates Court. I'll deal with that rather than getting a barrister.'

Matt was willing to take the case. It seemed like fate; his father had helped me during my first case and now Matt would help me clear my name a second time. I trusted Matt and made the decision there and then to hire him as my solicitor.

When I returned home, I wrote to the Police Federation requesting that Matt Foot and his firm represent me and asked for continued funding for my case. As I had suspected, the Police Federation responded by declining to financially support me. However, knowing that I had a legal team that I could trust gave me a much-needed boost. In the weeks leading up to the summons date, I tried to gather as much support as possible.

On Friday 2 May 2014, after weeks of trying to organise a meeting, I finally met with Janet Hills and Bevan Powell from the Black Police Association (BPA). Janet was a detective sergeant and the first black female chair of the BPA, while Bevan had recently retired from the Met. We met at a small coffee shop in Hammersmith.

I thanked both officers for offering to meet with me and explained my current situation. 'I retired from the police service two years ago, and they are still coming at me.'

'Don't worry,' Janet told me. 'If it was serious they would have arrested you rather than serving a summons on you.'

'It is worrying when they get people to say such things about something that happened in 1986,' I responded. 'They are pursuing me in retirement. I feel like they're shutting down those who stand up to the establishment.'

'How's the council?' Bevan queried, trying to change the subject.

'Difficult. I've gone from one corrupt organisation to another.'

Bevan tried to be encouraging: 'Keep your head down. You are letting others attack you.'

'If I did that we'd all be back in the '60s, being discriminated and abused,' I responded.

Bevan looked uneasy. 'I appreciate what you're saying, but there are other ways to deal with matters.'

'By selling your soul? I'm not part of that culture and never will be.'

'Gurpal, is there any truth in the allegations?' asked Janet. Her question stung.

'How can you ask that? Do I have to remind you about how you were treated by Operation Trident?'

Janet, a black policer officer, claimed that she had been denied a fair hearing after missing out on an intelligence job with Operation Trident, which was investigating shootings in London's black communities. After Janet accused Scotland Yard of racial discrimination, senior officers said it would be illegal to explain why she had not secured the job. In the Court of Appeal, Janet was told that she had failed the vetting process, but Janet was keen to find out the reason why. Lord Justice John Mummery responded that Janet had already been given a reason.

'You want reasons for the reasons,' he told her counsel.

The appeal judges ruled that the employment tribunal had been wrong to order the Met to show Janet confidential documents covering her job application. They said Janet, who had been with the Met since 1991, claimed racial discrimination after being rejected for the job, which went to a white officer. Janet said she was told by Chief Superintendent John Coles, head of the new unit: 'It is inappropriate for you to join Trident. I can't tell you why.'

I left the meeting disappointed. I had been a member of

the BPA for years, and had always tried to help fellow officers, working tirelessly with staff associations to support those discriminated against. I settled several cases out of court by negotiating with senior officers. I felt there was no reciprocation. Another dead end.

I reflected on the beginnings of the BPA. In March 1988, I attended a meeting at Bramshill Police College, led by senior white police officers, to discuss ethnicity in the police and how to improve recruitment from ethnic communities. Recruitment figures were improving but there was a serious haemorrhage as ethnic minority officers were leaving in droves. Also in attendance was Detective Sergeant Norwell Roberts (Gumbs), the first black officer to join the Met in 1967, and Constable Leslie Bowie, who joined the police in 1973 and took the Met to an employment tribunal in 1999 after being denied promotion. It was a good meeting, with full and frank discussions, and ended with an agreement that it was possible for all ethnic minority officers to be consulted on how they were treated in the Met and a plan on how to keep ethnic minority officers who were leaving within five years' service.

Looking back, this meeting was the foundation stone for the BPA and all other staff associations to provide a forum of support and guidance for ethnic minority officers. Many would say the Black Police Association was formed as a result of the seminars held at Bristol University in July 1990 – how wrong is that perception?

As I walked to the station to get the Tube home, I picked

up a copy of the *Evening Standard*, which had an article about a DPS officer in the Met who'd been allowed to retire and keep his pension without facing criminal action. Detective Constable Alex Manz had been sacked over allegations that he sexually assaulted two women. He was arrested in January 2013 as part of an IPCC supervised investigation but the DPS had issued no press release about the case. Was this not yet another example of institutional racism?

Over the coming days, several local papers, including the *Hounslow Chronicle* and the established Punjabi paper *Des Pardes*, published articles about me. The majority of them were negative, although some articles hinted at my previous history with the Met. I just hoped people would try to look me up, make sensible links and see what was happening. The more coverage my story got the more people I reached, but there were still pros and cons to the newspaper articles. I received many calls of support and visits from friends and relatives, which was nice, although still difficult, but it wasn't nice having ghastly, vile lies written about me. And it wasn't easy for my family either.

●　●　●

On Saturday 3 May, Sathat, who was still in a state of shock, met with Darshan Nagra, the Cranford ward chairman and a local elder whom I respected. He informed us that only new leaflets would now be used for the election campaign and the old ones would be discarded. The new Labour Party leaflets had a photograph of the other two candidates and I no longer existed. More rejection – more people assuming I was guilty.

When we returned home, I received a call from the general secretary of the ward, asking me to attend a meeting at a neighbour's home. The meeting was attended by the elder Asian Labour Party members who told me to campaign only in an adjoined estate within the Cranford ward and not locally. I said they were making a terrible mistake. They were convicting me of something that I hadn't done. I reminded them of injustices committed by the police against Asians, before getting up to leave. Another slap in the face; another door closed. The unfairness and injustice infuriated me. I had done nothing wrong. People were tying the noose around my neck before knowing the truth. Events were spiralling out of control.

Back home a letter was waiting for me. I recognised the printed logo; it was from Lord Singh of Wimbledon. I opened the letter with trepidation, but was pleasantly surprised to learn that Lord Singh had written to the Commissioner, Sir Bernard Hogan-Howe, in support of me. At least some people could see what was happening and backed me. I hadn't lost faith in humanity just yet.

That evening, Sathat and I were on a walk when I hit on the idea of getting T-shirts to publicise my candidacy as an independent for the elections. I designed a simple message to go across the shirts and the next day placed an order with Vista Print.

It was a rollercoaster experience: so many ups and downs,

though definitely more downs. People at the Met were seeking to discredit me and I learnt that some local people were also trying to cash in on my misfortune. Mr Nagra called to inform me that one of the other candidates, Sangha, and his friend, an ex-councillor, and hired help, were campaigning and visiting local residents with the damning press releases, encouraging people not to vote for me. People were clearly capitalising on my misfortune. To add insult to injury, I heard that the local Sikh Gurdwara was delivering a similar message to the Sikh community, actively discouraging people to vote for me and instead to vote for 'proper' turban-wearing Sikh candidates.

During my campaign, my tactic was to be open and honest. I found that if I explained what was happening and related my history with the Met, people were understanding and sympathetic. To rally support, Sathat and I went to see John McDonnell, the MP for Hayes and Harlington and a good friend who had always offered his support. We met John on Friday 9 May at his office. He was shocked and disgusted. I felt it was a productive meeting as he offered to arrange a cross-party meeting to discuss my situation. He also advised me to invite Matt Foot to the meeting.

When I got home, I logged on to my computer to check emails and have a scroll through the news. A headline by Labour 25, an unofficial website aimed at covering political scandal, caught my eye: 'The Labour Party candidate in the Hounslow council elections Gurpal Virdi has been accused of raping a child.' The media coverage had taken a turn for the worse, as the charge was never rape.

I received more bad news in the form of a phone call from Matt – my request for legal aid had been denied. Undeterred, I decided to put in an appeal for the funds, only to receive a call from the Police Federation a few weeks later, who were again declining to support my request for legal funding.

On Thursday 22 May, the day of the local elections, I rose early and visited all the polling stations. I spent most of the day meeting and greeting voters outside polling stations and was joined by Sathat and Kesar. Then, on Friday, Sathat, Nagra and I went to the civic centre to watch the count. It was a slow, nerve-wracking day, waiting for all of the votes to be counted and verified. By late afternoon, we were told that the results were ready to be announced. I was nervous – this was something that I really wanted. I took Sathat's hand and we stood anxiously waiting for the results to be read. It soon became apparent that I had achieved a substantial number of votes, double the amount that the Conservative candidate had received, and I was duly elected as an independent councillor for Cranford ward.

When we finally arrived home, we were exhausted, but happily enjoyed a few beers with family and close friends. I was ecstatic – I had beaten the odds. Despite the Labour Party turning its back on me and the Met releasing a damning press release, the local community had kept their faith and this gave me the confidence I needed to continue the fight to clear my name.

CHAPTER 9

ESTABLISHING
THE FACTS

My election high was quickly dampened by the Met
continuing to feed press releases to the media. The following appeared on the Met's website:

> **Former officer summonsed for indecent assault on boy**
> Former MPS officer, Gurpal Virdi, (DOB 07/09/58) of
> Hounslow, has been summoned to appear on 30/05/14
> before Westminster Magistrates' Court to answer to:
>
> Offence: Between 30/09/1986 and 31/12/1986 within the
> Jurisdiction of the Central Criminal Court, Mr Gurpal
> Virdi, being a Public Officer, namely a Metropolitan police
> officer, and acting as such, without reasonable excuses
> or justification, wilfully misconducted himself to such a
> degree as to amount to an abuse of the public's trust in that
> office. (Contrary to Common Law)
>
> Offence: Indecent assault on a boy under the age of six-
> teen years (Section fifteen of the Sexual Offences Act 1956)
>
> Particulars: Between 30/09/86 and 31/12/1986 within

the jurisdiction of the CCC you indecently assaulted a boy under sixteen.

The summons follows an investigation by the Directorate of Professional Standards into an allegation of an historical indecent assault of a male prisoner.

Source: Metropolitan Police Service

• • •

On the day of the court hearing, Friday 30 May, I met Matt at a coffee shop near Edgware Road Tube station. He explained what would happen in court, but, having been a police officer, I was already very familiar with proceedings. After arriving at court, we discovered that my case was not on the official display list that detailed which cases would be heard on that day. While in the waiting area, Ben Owusu, a member of the Independent Advisory Group (IAG), came and sat next to me. Ben told me about a Gold Group that had been set up by the Met. A Gold Group is a regularly held meeting where officers oversee a specific police investigation. It is designed to improve the way police respond during investigations and must be led by an officer ranked as a commander or above.

Ben told me that the group had met on 28 May and discussed Sathat's and Peter's letters to the Commissioner as well as my FoIA (Freedom of Information Act) request. Ben also informed me that DI Donna Smith was the investigating officer; DCI Tim Neligan the SIO (Senior Investigation

Officer); while Chief Superintendent Alaric Bonthron and Deputy Assistant Commissioner Fiona Taylor were in charge of the DPS at the meeting. The types of questions that were asked by IAG members included: Why now? How many officers have gone through this? How many in the van? Ben was hesitant to give me the answers.

He also told me the IAG had met the commissioner and his deputy ten days after the initial press release, and that the operation was being conducted by Sapphire and DPS. The Gold Group had no background history or previous knowledge of the case in 1998 and the complainant had come forward fourteen months earlier.

Despite the case not being listed, we were called in person by the court usher to enter the courtroom. As Matt and I entered, I was asked to step into the dock, which was a plastic cage. The hearing was very brief. I confirmed my name, address and entered a plea of not guilty. When the prosecution gave details of the case, even the magistrate expressed concern that the case was twenty-seven years old. The case was then passed on to Southwark Crown Court for 12 June. The prosecution wanted to add bail conditions, but the magistrate refused and granted me unconditional bail. As we left the court, I pointed out DC Gadsby to Ben, because I wanted to see his reaction. It appeared that they knew each other, which confirmed my suspicions that Ben was only speaking to me so that he could gather information for the Met.

A media pack was outside the court. I understood they had a job to do, so I let them photograph me. But I said nothing to reporters as we headed back to the café, where we read the summary of the case provided by the CPS. The summary contained accounts by additional witnesses:

Danny Dwyer's account (retired detective sergeant)

Dwyer was a police officer between 1981 and 2011. From 1986 to 1989 he worked on the Divisional crime squad. He named several officers he'd worked with, including me, and explained that officers would be partnered for a few months before being rotated to a different pairing. He remembered me as a pleasant person.

Dwyer thought I was racist towards black people and recalled an incident when a black youth had spat in our direction. Apparently, I'd overreacted and called the youth 'a dirty black bastard' then forced him against a wall. Dwyer said he'd pulled me off and calmed the situation. Dwyer had never seen me with an ASP.

David Zinzan (retired assistant chief constable, Devon and Cornwall)

Zinzan had no knowledge of the attack on Mr Anqkar. He said I'd had an aggressive manner and would often escalate situations in order to make arrests for public order offences. He described me as confrontational and particularly negative towards Africans. To his knowledge, no members of the crime squad had carried an ASP. In fact, the first time he had seen one had been in 1997.

Linda Taylor (Mr Anqkar's partner)

Ms Taylor said she met Wasim Anqkar – known to her as Harry – in the late '80s. About two years into their relationship he said he had been arrested. He said there had been a fight inside the police van and he had kicked the van doors open.

'At the time he told me, I just thought he'd been a naughty boy when he was younger, and I didn't think any more of it,' she said.

About five years later, he'd told her more about the incident.

'Harry told me that during this fight with the police one of the officers put a truncheon up his bum through his shell bottoms. He said this officer, who he called George, was trying to make him a grass and would often pick him up in St Johns Hill in front of his friends … He told me another officer called Tom had told George to stop. Harry told them he was fifteen. His dad came to the station and he was cautioned.'

Gehazi Sautelabaap (Mr Anqkar's father)

Mr Sautelabaap recalled collecting Harry from the station but did not recall his son talking about a sexual or physical assault.

I was disappointed that Zinzan had been recruited as a police witnesses; I'd hoped he would support me. I had trusted

Zinzan. He had attended my wedding and Sathat had supported him after he split up with his girlfriend. I felt hurt.

My court hearing was on the lunchtime and 6.30 p.m. BBC London News. Later that evening, I did some research on the ASP and sent a newspaper article from *The Independent* dated 21 June 1994 to Matt. It read:

The baton was tested by thirteen forces between March and May. A further month's trial of alternative models is taking place in three forces, including the Met. The results will be considered by the Association of Chief Police Officers next month.

Avon and Somerset Police became the first force to start using replacements in January, choosing the ASP, a straight metal baton which extends from 7in to 21in.

As I'd said in my interview with the police, no ASPs were available during the time of the alleged assault. This article proved Anqkar had not told the truth.

Matt also requested further background information. This included details regarding the previous employment tribunal with the Met, copies of my police commendations and other achievements. A few days after the court hearing, the television journalist Simon Israel from Channel 4 contacted me about the case and *The Guardian*'s Vikram Dodd was also interested.

Remarkably, just as had happened back in 1998, during the first case, our telephone line had become faulty again.

I always suspected that the telephone lines had been tapped, but this was denied by the Met. Personally, I wasn't convinced and I suspected the police were listening in to my conversations.

On Thursday 12 June, Matt and I headed for Southwark Crown Court for the second court hearing. Once again, upon entering the courtroom, I was asked to enter a glass cage.

It is a horrible feeling to be put in a glass cage, as if you are a serial killer or terrorist. The clear plastic makes it extremely difficult to hear court proceedings, and I was unable to hear what was going on. I repeatedly asked the clerk to repeat what was being said. It was a short preliminary hearing even though the Met's barrister, Jeremy Randle, tried to convey the seriousness of the allegations and request strict bail conditions to be imposed on me. However, the judge once again granted me unconditional bail.

Following the hearing, and back at home, I started my own investigation. I dug up my old paperwork and researched police procedures during the 1980s. I found my old instruction manual and general orders regarding procedures in the '80s, which I sent to Matt. Then I made calls and wrote emails to people I'd known in the community during that period. While carrying out my investigations, I attempted to contact Godfrey Cremer, who had worked at the Ealing Racial Equality Unit while I had been posted at Ealing and had supported me during my first case. I had hoped he would be able to take to the stand as a witness for the defence, but I was met with the news that he had passed away from cancer in 2012. Hearing news of his death was both greatly saddening and disappointing.

Some days later, I contacted my old boss Tarique Ghaffur's company to request a meeting with him. A former assistant commissioner at the Met, Tarique had facilitated my entrance into the Met in 2002, after I was reinstated as an officer. I had always admired Tarique and his progression through the force. Born in Uganda, Tarique immigrated to Britain in 1972, after President Idi Amin expelled most of Uganda's minority South Asian population. In 1974, he joined the Greater Manchester Police, one of two ethnic minority officers in a force with over 6,000 officers.

Tarique transferred to the Met in 1999 as a deputy assistant commissioner and in 2000 served as borough commander of the City of Westminster. This was following the damming Stephen Lawrence report that labelled the Met as institutionally racist. Unfortunately, despite his initial support in 2002, I didn't receive a response from Tarique. This was yet another dead end.

Following this disappointment, I was contacted by Ali Dizaei on 25 June, urging me to contact him as he had important information regarding my case. Ali was a fellow Asian police officer in the Met, who had achieved commander rank, but also suffered from racial discrimination during his career. I quickly responded via email and asked what information he had, and he told me that he knew of somebody who could provide important information in support of my innocence. Despite having slight reservations, I asked Ali to pass my contact details to this person and waited for them to get in touch.

On Friday 27 June, I received a call. The man introduced himself as Michael Doherty, a name I was familiar with, and he claimed that he had also been a victim of malicious prosecutions by the police and the DPS. He said that he had heard of my case due to recent press coverage, and that he had recently been contacted by a man called Anqkar, was in possession of a recording of a conversation with him and that he wanted to pass this to my solicitor. I was suspicious because I thought it might be another trap. Nonetheless, I thought this was worth pursuing and provided him with Matt's contact details.

After I hung up, I emailed Matt about the call I had just received and also contacted Michael's MP, John McDonnell, who confirmed that Michael was reliable. Once this reliability was determined, Matt called Michael.

Michael explained to Matt that Anqkar had said that he had no faith in the police because he knew that they could turn against him at any given moment. He went on to explain that it was his brother-in-law, Tom Todd, who suggested that Anqkar speak with Michael, as he was aware of his reputation of exposing police corruption. Anqkar went on to state that despite having spoken to close to twenty solicitors, no one was willing to take his case – and he was keen to establish his own legal team who would look after his own interests.

In addition to looking for legal representation, Anqkar

also said that he had consulted with a private doctor and was now seeking counselling and therapy.

Matt also made the following notes from his call:

Re: Gurpal Virdi
30 June 2014, 5.15 p.m.
Birnberg Peirce
Michael Doherty (MD); Matt Foot (MF).

MD: 'I got a Facebook message from someone called Tom Todd, who sent a link to an article on the Gurpal Virdi case. I got this message and we had a bit of a conversation; I actually told the guy it might be a stitch up. He added me as a friend in November but I don't know who he is. I said I knew he (Gurpal) was standing for election and that before all the allegations he put out a press release saying he'd tackle corruption in the council and local police – sorry, not tackle corruption, hold them to account.'

MF: 'Why would people come to you?'

MD: 'I think I've been quite open about the fact I'm trying to change the Met and its failure to actually hold the police to account, but I really don't know. People aren't asking me for anything they just want to tell me. I don't know if they're trying to misinform; I guess that's something you'll have to look at, but certainly from what the person said it just doesn't sound right. I'm highly suspicious of the case myself. I know the Met didn't introduce collapsible truncheons until the '90s, so things don't add up.

They tried to call me a number of times, that's the number on the thing – it's apparently the person's number. I didn't answer the call that evening. Then, I think it was the next day, I spoke to them … I tried to call him back twice and then he called me again and I spoke to him for about forty minutes. The BLC one must be the original file and then it's converted to MP3.'

MF: 'What does it say?'

MD: 'It's a forty-minute conversation and he explains what's supposed to have happened in the back of the van, where he's hit with a retractable type of truncheon and another officer tells Gurpal Virdi to stop, and then he shoves this truncheon up his anus through his trousers. Then he starts talking about the investigation and how the police weren't really interested too much in the allegations until they found out who the officer was and then they really wanted to get him. He talks about the police commissioner travelling abroad to meet the officer giving evidence, and about how the officer has immunity from prosecution.'

MF: 'How was it left?

MD: 'I said something about "what do you want from me?" He started talking about a civil claim and I said I could send him some details of solicitors that …'

MF: 'Civil claim against who?

MD: 'The Met. I could send names of solicitors and he could speak to them and see what they think. I'm sick and tired of the Met playing stupid games with the criminal justice system and running good coppers down. They try and portray me like I'm a police hater or something, but if I think an officer's been done an injustice I'm more than happy to help them. I was involved with Danny Major, another case where an officer got stitched up, and I watched the Ali Dizaei trial and it was very, very suspicious.

There's this double standard two headed complaint system, where you castigate good officers who speak out and protect the corrupt ones at the expense of the public, and I think it's blatantly obvious what's going on. I don't know any more about the case than I've been told, but just from that it sounds farcical: a thirty-year-old allegation. And I know how they play with the papers; I've had it myself with the local press. These articles go out and you're smeared irrespective of whether you're innocent.

I know a fair bit about criminal law now and I certainly don't think victims would in any other circumstances know what's going on inside the investigation. It's not appropriate that they would know someone has been given immunity. Or that the commissioner travelled abroad to get a statement. I just don't think it's right whether it's the defence or the prosecution. I'm not a 'grass'; I don't know if this is a set up because I do get people talking to me about their cases and most of them sound genuine in terms of allegations that have been made and stuff like that. I don't know the case but you can see it's dodgy. Lots of police officers speak up for what they saw and next thing they have their legs cut from under them and they're out.'

Following Matt's conversation with Michael, he asked to meet with me outside the British Library to talk about the call. Matt recalled what had been discussed with Michael, and said that he wasn't too convinced by what he had been told. I was hoping that this may have helped my case but Matt's reluctance had left me deflated. Unable to sleep that night, I went downstairs, made a cup of tea, switched on the computer and Googled Michael Doherty.

I discovered he was a father of three, with a respectable job as an aircraft engineer. He had challenged the system in August 2008, after discovering a long series of messages between a thirteen-year-old child and someone who appeared to be grooming her. The messages were sexually explicit. At one point the person proposed staging a kidnap and whisking her away. Michael went to the police with an 86-page dossier and later phoned Hillingdon station five times to speak to a senior officer, to find out why, in his view, the investigation seemed to have stalled.

Several days later, two officers arrived at Michael's house to arrest him. Amongst other charges, they claimed Michael had harassed Tracey Murphy, the secretary to Hillingdon Borough Commander Carl Bussey. She claimed Michael had phoned ten times in two days and had been 'abusive' as well as 'rude and aggressive'. Michael offered to get dressed and go to the station, but the officers handcuffed him and then dragged him out of the house in his dressing gown.

At the same time, the police dropped the grooming investigation. They had not examined the child's computer. A note by a detective inspector at Hillingdon station later justified the police action by maintaining 'there is no evidence of a crime capable of proof'.

Michael had proof his calls to Tracey Murphy were neither abusive nor aggressive because he had recorded them. The recordings proved he had remained controlled, patient and polite. But the police failed to pass the recordings to the Crown Prosecution Service, so Michael was charged. In court, Tracey Murphy admitted her recollection of the calls was hazy and Michael was acquitted. He then reported the matter to the Independent Police Complaints Commission.

The IPCC failed to act against any police officers or Tracey Murphy. In what is believed to be the first time in UK legal history that an individual launched a private prosecution against a police civilian worker, Michael then tried to bring a private prosecution against Tracey Murphy for perverting the course of justice, but it was not proceeded with.

He also began a private prosecution against the two officers who arrested him at his home. Sergeant Gareth Blackburn and Detective Constable Stephen MacDonald were summoned to appear in court to face charges of affray, burglary, aggravated burglary, misconduct in public office, kidnap and false imprisonment. The statement of offence alleged they were trespassers who refused to leave Michael's home and attempted to inflict grievous bodily harm. The final result was not available on the internet, but I later discovered that these charges were likewise not proceeded with.

After researching Michael that evening, I believed that

there could be truth in his account, and his willingness to help restored hope that I might have the evidence to fight the false allegations in court. I made a note to revisit this with Matt as soon as possible and Matt also agreed to pursue this line of enquiry further, once Michael had released the actual recording of the conversation between himself and Anqkar.

Meanwhile, we had been waiting for further disclosure from the prosecution, which, according to Southwark Crown Court directions, should have been released to me and my legal team on 24 July. Yet, 24 July came and went and we heard nothing; it was deeply frustrating and infuriating. Three days later and we were still waiting on the further disclosure – the prosecution were directly flouting court directions so I asked Matt to escalate the matter.

By the end of the month, nothing had been received. However, on 31 July, Sathat received a response from the Chief Crown Prosecutor of London, Ms Baljit Ubhey, in response to a complaint she had sent to the CPS regarding the allegations and lack of evidence. Ubhey responded:

> I can confirm that the case involving your husband has been carefully reviewed in accordance with the Code. I am, however, unable to go into detail about the evidence in the case as proceedings are live. I am also unable to comment on content that does not specifically relate to the CPS.

Sir Peter Bottomley also received a response to his concerns regarding the prosecutions and the implications of its failure.

The response was from Peter Lewis, chief executive of the CPS:

> You have asked that in the event this prosecution is withdrawn or fails, that I assess the reasons for the unsuccessful outcome. Ms Baljit Ubhey, the chief prosecutor for CPS London is responsible for the quality of casework and decision making in London. Under her lead, please be assured that if this case results in an unsuccessful outcome for the prosecution, the reasons will be analysed, as they are for all unsuccessful prosecutions. I will write to you again at the conclusion of this case.

It seemed that the CPS were unwilling to give any tangible insight into the case, despite numerous complaints and concerns raised. I was not surprised.

With the very little information available, I had to continue my investigation and was exploring all sorts of avenues, to get anything that might help me in my defence. This included submitting a request for information regarding the number of ethnic minority officers that had joined the Met since 1967. However, I received a refusal to provide the requested information.

I also started to make my own enquiries into Wasim Anqkar. Through online research, I learnt that he had been involved in a bankruptcy case in 2004. His trading company name was Oat Drivers. I also discovered, through a search on ancestry.com, that in 1991 he had been married to Leah

Caraboo – not Linda Taylor, who he claimed had been his partner since the late 1980s. I decided to order a copy of their marriage certificate as I knew it would be important evidence in helping us build a case against Anqkar.

Anqkar's bankruptcy and marriage documents confirmed his date of birth as 29 August 1970. The police report stated the same date of birth. Why, then, did Anqkar claim to be fifteen years old at the time of the allegations, when he was clearly sixteen at the time?

As the police report had the correct date of birth, it was clear the DPS had been aware of his age at the time of the allegations. Yet the press release they issued to the media stated that Anqkar was under sixteen. It was obvious to me at this point that the media coverage and press releases had clearly been designed to create a maximum negative impact against me, at a time when I was seeking election as a local councillor. The age of consent in the UK is sixteen, so if you are reporting a sexual offences allegation, the offence is immediately much more serious if the victim was under sixteen when the alleged incident occurred.

Meanwhile, on 28 August 2014, I attended Southwark Crown Court again with Matt and Henry Blaxland QC, for a Plea and Case Management hearing. Matt had worked with Henry on several cases and assured me that he would be a suitable barrister to represent me during trial proceedings.

I was asked to put forward a plea, but was advised by my legal team to not do so on the basis that we had not received a full disclosure of documentation by the MPS/CPS as previously advised by the court.

At this same hearing, my legal team submitted an application for the case to be dismissed. The hearing for this dismissal was set by the judge to be heard on Monday 29 September 2014 at Southwark Crown Court. The prosecution served Henry with a new draft indictment with the offences amended – the charges were amended and the court conceded that Anqkar had not been younger than sixteen years of age at the time of the alleged attack. This was useful for my defence, because it began to highlight the incompetence of the prosecution's investigation.

Upon reviewing the new indictment, it was apparent that the CPS had amended the charges to include indecent assault on a male, misconduct in public office and actual bodily harm (ABH). I would now face three charges relating to the same incident (I saw this as basically throwing mud at me and hoping some would stick). This further exacerbated the concerns that both my legal team and I had about the case going ahead.

Even though the indictment had been amended and that reference to Anqkar being under sixteen had now been amended, the damage had been done. I was still unable to get fully involved with my voluntary work and council duties. The MPS had known Wasim Anqkar's date of birth, yet when they interviewed me and told me he was under sixteen, they had done so deliberately. Their actions went beyond incompetence. Such officers should not have been serving in the MPS.

Following this amendment, I submitted a complaint to the Independent Police Complaints Commission about the deliberate discrepancy about the age, the press releases and the associated negative publicity. But I didn't hold any hope that my complaint would be investigated. The following day an article appeared online with the headline: 'Hounslow councillor and ex-detective applies for historic assault charge to be dismissed'.

The DPS was continuing to leak information to the media.

CHAPTER 10

TAPED CONVERSATION

At the end of August, Matt called to tell me he had received the recording of the conversation between Michael Doherty and Anqkar. Anqkar had called Doherty for advice on suing the police and volunteered during the call that he intended to do so. Below is a full transcript of that conversation, which starts with Anqkar telling Michael that his brother-in-law, Tom Todd, has suggested that he get in contact:

MD: 'Alright, OK. I know he has been following me online, is he a friend of yours?'

WA: 'Yeah, a good friend of mine.'

MD: 'What's happening then? Obviously what I do, as you know, is deal with police corruption issues and stuff like that, private prosecutions of the Met police officers and that type of thing.'

WA: 'Well, I don't know if you know a police officer called Gurpal Virdi?'

MD: 'I've seen the case online and stuff, yeah.'

WA: 'I'm the guy involved in that case there yeah. 1985,

when I was fifteen years old, he arrested me for, what's it, having an offensive weapon.'

MD: 'OK.'

WA: 'He put me in a van with another police officer.'

MD: 'Uh huh.'

WA: 'A guy named Tom and, um, what's it, as soon as he got me in the van he, when he arrested me he never asked me my name or age, OK?'

MD: 'Yeah.'

WA: 'So they put me in the van, he handcuffed me while I was in the van. As soon as the door was shut and the hand-cuffs were on, he asked me my name. He said, "What's your name?" I said: "Harry Anqkar." He goes: "What kind of name is that for a fucking nigger?" Slapped me straight in the face and then he started bashing me up – I mean big time, like big time. He started bashing me up in the van.'

MD: 'He's like retired now isn't he? He is a retired police officer?'

WA: 'Yes, he's a councillor now isn't he? He's a Labour councillor for um… Hounslow.'

MD: 'Is that the same area where the incident happened?'

WA: 'No, this happened in Battersea. St John's Hill. OK … the beating started at the Granada Bingo Hall off St John's Hill and, what's it, it carried on all the way down to Clapham Junction. It must have been about five beatings, yeah. At this time, the other officer, as soon as the beating started, the other officer started protesting: "Get the fuck off him! Leave him alone! Get off him – you're killing him!

Fucking hell, George – get off him, man! This is the last time; I've fucking had enough. George, leave him alone." Continuously protesting, yeah. Now, being younger, I thought this was a what's it, serious case of bad cop good cop, not understanding the situation you know.'

MD: 'Gurpal was a young cop at the time or a new cop?'

WA: 'He was about twenty-six. He'd been in the force for four years. He started in 1982 and this was 1986, so he was about twenty-six years old.'

MD: 'Why do you think he would? Why would he do that? Why did he do that, is he a racist or something? Racist or something?'

WA: 'I think he's got a racist element about him. He's got a racist element about him, but the plot thickens as to the reason why he's done it, OK? Which I didn't understand at the time, but I think becomes more apparent as we go along, yeah. He's a very weak man and I was a strong youth, yeah. I couldn't understand how he was giving me so much pain, it was like in the back of that van. I was like a pinball in the back of that van. I kept being thrown all over the place, yeah. But what it was, he had a collapsible truncheon.'

MD: 'OK.'

WA: 'And he was using it to hit my pressure points and I don't know if you've ever been hit by something like that very, very...'

MD: 'Yeah, yeah.'

WA: 'Do you know what I mean? It makes you, put it this way, it makes you jump like a dog when it hits you ... You yelp like a dog … as soon as it has contact with you. So in the end, he wore me down. He had me in a position where he was sitting on his arse … he was sitting in a rowing position, yeah, with his legs and feet on my shoulder, pulling the handcuffs so [that] I was on my back with my arms fully extended. He was pulling on my handcuffs, so, you know, in the end I had the pain of the handcuffs and being so tired, I sort of like nearly passed out … So I can remember the attacks stopped for about a minute, OK … I came off my back, on to my side and went into a foetal position, OK. And what he done, he came round, I thought he was picking me up by the waist, yeah, but he wasn't, he actually pinned me down with his armpit and his arm.'

MD: 'Right.'

WA: 'Got the truncheon and stuck it up my backside.'

MD: 'No way!'

WA: 'Straight through. He never pulled down my trousers or anything; I had a pair of shell bottoms on.'

MD: 'OK.'

WA: 'Yeah. Really thin material, so basically he's pushed it up my backside. I was in so much pain. I was on my side still and all I could do was scream and kick out, so I started kicking. I was down by the doors and I started kicking the doors and they flew open … The other policeman banged on the wall and he got the other police officer to stop the van run around and shut the door.'

MD: 'There were three cops in the van? Him…'

WA: 'There were three.'

MD: 'And two others.'

WA: 'Yeah, so you got Tom and George in the back with me and the driver, yeah.'

MD: 'Alright, what was it like? The old Sherpa vans or…'

WA: 'Yes, old Sherpa, exactly. Old Sherpa, yeah. One little light that was very dim, you understand? I managed to kick the doors open, the van stops, get to a standstill and like just as at the Clapham Junction, Falcon Road runs along parallel. There was a bus stop. I looked up, yeah, and I saw about twenty faces staring into the van. I looked across at George and that's when I saw the weapon in his hand. He just pulled it out. The shock of the door opening up, he just pulled it out of my backside. You understand that's when I first saw it. I never saw it until then, but that's when I first saw it.'

MD: 'Did any of them report that at the time, or did they … What did they do, the ones, the cop in the back of the van?'

WA: 'The three cops in the back of the van never reported nothing. The one in the front he never reported nothing, nobody.'

MD: 'Anything when you get to the police station? Like recording injuries or anything like that?'

WA: 'To be honest, he knew exactly what he was doing. I had no facial injuries, OK. All it was bruising to the body, where he'd used his – what's it – truncheon. You know, hit my pressure points. The only injuries I had was serious swelling of [my] wrists by being dragged around in the van with the handcuffs. That's the only, what's it, injury you could actually see.'

MD: 'Did you report it? Getting at custody did you report it at custody or anything like that?'

WA: 'No, I never reported it at custody; never reported at custody. I was terrified, man. I was fifteen years old.'

MD: 'How did it come out like now, or...'

WA: 'Right, OK, let's get over this part. So, as I said to them, when I pulled the underclothes out of my backside I said I can't believe you just done that to a fifteen-year-old kid.'

MD: 'Yeah, when they get to the police station they have to call an appropriate adult, yeah?'

WA: 'Exactly, so I said as soon as my dad comes in here, as soon as I get interviewed, I'm going to tell my dad what's happened on tape; you understand? ... Tom and George are both standing there, pulling sadistic faces – do you understand? – at the cell door. I managed to walk up to them. I done quite a swift move. I used to be a basketball player so I've done a one-two step; I stepped towards them and I stepped away from them, back into the cell. They tried to drag me out of the cell and give me another good hiding, yeah, but what I done, I left my jacket behind. I took my jacket off, yeah, and then just threw my jacket in and shut the door.

I was in there about two hours, OK, and they brought me out and what they done they, what's it, fingerprinted me, and took my picture and said, what's it, you're ready to go, and I said: "OK, then." I said: "I thought I was ready to go for interview." I said: "Is my dad here?" They said:

"Yeah, your dad's outside." So all of a sudden they've just fucking, what's it, released me into my dad's custody.'

MD: 'What was the alleged offensive weapon?'

WA: 'A knife; knife; work knife.'

MD: 'OK.'

WA: 'I had an altercation with somebody, that's how the knife came out you see. When they actually approached me, the knife was already dropped on the floor, so they picked the knife up and they … you know, what's it, put it in a bag or whatever, and when I got in the van I never had no knife on me, yeah.

My dad said he did believe me, but he didn't know how to handle it, because he was having immigration problems and he didn't want to cause no hassle for himself, you understand? So he just ignored what I've said … about a week later, OK, George has come back round my area, OK, where I got arrested and he arrested me for driving a car that I was not driving. OK, so he put me in the van and said: "You're under sixteen and can't drive a car." I said: "I wasn't driving." He said: "You're nicked anyway. You're coming to the police station."

… He continued to harass me on a daily basis; coming round my area; picking me up in his car; dropping me off outside bookies offices, where other black people could see me getting out of a police car – what he wanted, he wanted me to become an informer. He [GV] promised I would get, what's it, a brown envelope every month with money.'

MD: 'It happens. Yeah, it happens.'

WA: 'So, about a month after that, I got a summons through the post summoning me to attend Balham Juvenile Court for the offensive weapon. So I went to court. Eventually, I got a fine ... I mentioned to my solicitor that he beat me up in the back of the van. I was too embarrassed to talk about the indecent assault, yeah. So when I stood up to give my evidence, I mentioned it. I was frowned upon by the judge, she told me to shut up and don't say anything else about it, OK, and I was found guilty.'

MD: 'Is the judge still around?'

WA: 'I don't think she is. So basically I just carried on with my life, and then the harassment continued so, basically, I had to leave – my parents threw me out ... Got out of his jurisdiction and then never saw him or heard of him, OK, until about five years ago, OK. As I was driving down Tooting High Road, I saw this Indian guy around the market. I thought I know this guy, just from the back of his head I knew him, and I just thought to myself, he's still working – he's still a police officer. So I decided to put a complaint in. I went to Sapphire Unit, the rape unit, I put a complaint in to the police and they were like...'

MD: 'When was this? Five years ago?'

WA: 'No, this was a year and half ago.'

MD: 'OK.'

WA: 'You know, it took me a bit of time to pluck up the courage, you know what I mean? ... with the Jimmy Savile thing going on I was thinking yeah, well, if they investigate back thirty years I thought they wouldn't investigate, you understand, so basically I told them exactly what I told you. I said: "You find Tom [Makins] and he will admit to what happened."

So they found Tom, yeah, living abroad, OK. So Bernard Hogan-Howe and another officer jumped on a plane – I don't know where it is, all I know [is that] it was a long-haul flight, that's what the officer said yeah. I'm thinking Australia, Canada, one of them places, you know. So, they've gone out there, they've spoken to Tom, OK, and Tom has confirmed that I was beaten up in the back of the van. The words he used was "serious abuse of power" or something like that…'

MD: 'Well, there have been quite a few deaths in custody … especially around the Brixton area.'

WA: 'Yeah, they would have sat on me. They would have sat on me. They would have suffocated me.'

MD: 'Didn't you say Tom was at the cell door as well?'

WA: 'Yeah, growling, trying to terrify me, yeah. Because they knew what sort of trouble they were in, they didn't want me to talk so all that was to terrify me, you see what I mean? Terrorise me, [so I would] know not to talk. So yeah, he was at the cell door growling, yeah, he was there.

So I've told the police I don't want him prosecuted, I want him used as a witness. I want him to have immunity, OK. So they've gone over there and they've said: "Look, Mr Anqkar, he doesn't want you prosecuted." So Tom's opened his mouth, he's given a statement and said he's willing to come to court and say what happened.'

MD: 'Do you know when it's going to trial? Because I've seen in the papers that it will be in Southwark.'

WA: 'Yeah, it's in Southwark … the trial was set for the middle of October.'

MD: 'OK, well, I'll try and get down there to watch the trial as well. I mean are they, is it still the Sapphire Unit you're in touch with?'

WA: 'No … So it's actually Sir Bernard Hogan-Howe and the IPCC who actually brought this to prosecution, because, obviously, now I realise more about this officer, he's been a thorn in their backside for a long time.'

MD: 'Yeah, I mean there's quite a few reports about him. Isn't there like race discrimination and stuff like that?'

WA: 'That's it. He had about 300 grand out of them didn't he? For racial discrimination. He got sacked in 2000 or something and he got reinstated.'

MD: 'Yeah, yeah, I heard about that. How are the police with you now? Are they directing you to any solicitors or anything like that?'

WA: 'No, they haven't … I've got the CPS … that's not a barrister … I've got a solicitor sort of like keeping an eye on the case. You understand? A personal friend.'

MD: 'Oh, your own friend?'

WA: 'Yeah, yeah, he's a solicitor, keeping an eye on it … that's all I've got you know. I'm very dubious about the police anyway, you know what I mean, [given] the way that I've been treated in the past…'

MD: 'What about the IPCC? Are they not any help or anything like that?'

WA: 'Well they haven't. Since the whole thing started, I've had nothing in writing.'

…

MD: 'I mean you should go and speak to like, I don't know. I guess look at this going on like, a police action solicitor.'

WA: 'A what?'

MD: 'A police action solicitor. I mean are you thinking of suing the police or anything like that?'

WA: 'Oh God! I definitely want to sue the police, yeah. Yeah, definitely want to sue the police.'

MD: 'Have you spoken to any solicitors about it?'

WA: 'No, I haven't. No, because, to be honest, I'm under a psychiatrist at the moment. The whole incident, years ago, has given me some serious psychological problems, which I'm just sort of trying to get over now. Do you understand? So I'm under a psychiatrist. I've got to pay for that myself, £140 a month to go and see him. It's helping a little bit but … I've got some serious hate for the police. Every time I see them I feel rage, you understand?'

MD: 'It's understandable.'

WA: 'So I'm just trying to get that anger under control at the moment, before I do something stupid. You understand what I'm saying?'

MD: 'I know. I mean, a psychiatrist friend of mine does some work with the stuff I do that I can recommend you to. Have a think about these police action solicitors that I know. I could message you with some details and stuff about who you could speak to, if you want to go down that road – if you haven't already gone down that road. Get the trial out of the way. Isn't it in October?'

WA: 'Yeah, I just want justice to be done. It's taken twenty-nine years from when it happened and now, you understand, you know I'm a family man: I've got five kids now. You understand, you know.'

MD: 'It seems like they're taking it very seriously, the Metropolitan Police. Bernard Hogan-Howe actually physically went out there himself.'

WA: 'That's it, yeah. The commissioner himself went out there ... I don't know if you know a guy named PC Gadsby?'

MD: 'No, I don't know him.'

WA: 'He's from the IPCC, yeah. When they got back from wherever they went to go and see Tom, I see their attitude had totally changed. Whenever they were looking at me and saying: "Look, Mr Anqkar, you wasn't fifteen at the time, you were sixteen at the time it happened." I said: "I was on work experience, yeah, that's why I was in work clothes at the time, OK."'

...

MD: 'The bloke from IPCC actually told you that Hogan-Howe went with him?'

WA: 'Yeah.'

MD: 'Bloody hell.'

WA: 'No, my liaison officer, yeah, said that the commissioner went out there, you understand?'

MD: 'Well there's only one commissioner.'

WA: 'I think because he'd been a thorn in their side for a long time, I think that's why he's taken it up like this. But when they brought me to Brixton police station, what's it, the guy from the IPCC, he said Mr George Virdi is a seriously corrupt officer. He's got a file this big and he done a stack up with his hand, you know what I mean, and I thought: yeah, they know about this guy and they want him, you understand.'

MD: 'I mean the system of holding police to account, even if you've got good compelling evidence against them, in terms of racism cases ... only 1 per cent of those complaints were upheld. That is eight out of 8,000. So the fact is that you know top police officers ... who are abusing their position don't get held to account, so that they can continue doing the same sort of thing to other people throughout their career.'

WA: 'They will carry on. I mean even today it will carry on. Let me tell you this, my friend. Yeah I've lost a career over what he done. After I was arrested I never bathed for a year and half.'

MD: 'Never what?'

WA: 'I never had a bath for a year and half; I stunk like a dog. People could not understand it. When I finally did start bathing and I started getting my life together, I became, what's it, I became a commercial driver. Yeah, lorry driver.'

...

MD: 'Do you want me to think about a police actions so-licitor that you might want to speak to?'

WA: 'Yeah, please. Definitely.'

MD: 'Then they can speak to you.'

WA: 'I tell you what, do you think ... OK, right ... George Virdi, he will get a guilty?'

MD: 'I mean court's a funny funny business. You know, I guess it all depends on the evidence in the case, doesn't it? It depends on I guess the testimony of the police officer – you say who saw the stuff, what happened and all that, yeah.'

WA: 'All he can do is deny it, because basically, I'm just guessing here now, they've interviewed him under caution ... If he's come up with this big scenario that I attacked him in the back of the van, he disarmed me, you know, put me in handcuffs. All that could be blown out of the water, when he realises that Tom is making a statement.'

MD: 'Have they actually given him immunity from prose-cution, the other fella?'

WA: 'I believe so.'

MD: 'So he'll feel comfortable about saying whatever he has to say?'

WA: 'Exactly. Exactly. Let's say the court case goes ahead in October, he's found guilty, yeah, will the police still try and stop me from getting damages? Even though another police officer has admitted, yeah.'

MD: 'Look, how things work in a criminal trial is beyond

all reasonable doubt. A civil trial for damages is on the balance of probabilities.'

WA: 'OK, but do you think that… if I'm running a company and they've been found guilty of misconduct or whatever and, what's it, I would not put up a fight against [a] person claiming compensation.'

…

MD: 'Yeah, I guess so. I mean, in terms of if he said that you were beaten up in the back of the van and it wasn't right and stuff, yeah, I guess, well, that would be good evidence in a civil claim for damages against the Metropolitan Police, yeah.'

WA: 'This conversation is confidential between me and you.'

MD: 'Yeah, yeah, sure, sure.'

WA: 'OK, because I don't want something coming out in the trial so the trial gets messed up or anything – you know what I mean? You know, so it gets to trial. Michael, thank you. I'll be speaking to you again.'

CHAPTER 11

CASE FOR DISMISSAL

It was 29 September 2014, the day of the dismissal hearing.

Two weeks prior to the hearing, Henry received a bundle of documents from the CPS containing statements and interview notes from the investigation. With this new information in hand, Matt and I met with Henry, who was preparing his hearing argument for why the case should be dismissed. We ensured that the prosecution and the CPS had plenty of time to prepare.

Five days before the hearing, Henry received a single document. This was Anqkar's conviction certificate dated 23 July 1987, issued by Lambeth East Juvenile Court, which showed that on 31 October 1986 Anqkar was arrested for carrying an offensive weapon, and provoking a breach of the peace. It gave his date of birth as 29 August 1970, and the arresting officer as DC Markwick.

This marked a turning point in my defence. We were finally able to determine the date of Anqkar's arrest and therefore the date of the alleged assault. More importantly, I was NOT the arresting officer – a completely new name was introduced into the mix. Furthermore, the Met had had this certificate in their possession since 22 April 2013, although months earlier David Gadsby had claimed it had been destroyed. This was something that would require further investigation by myself and my team.

The dismissal hearing was held in Courtroom 15 at Southwark Crown Court. As I walked into the room I could see a number of familiar faces sat in the public gallery, including *Hounslow Chronicle* journalist Robert Cumber and MP Sir Peter Bottomley.

Just before the proceedings were set to begin, Matt told me that he had some news – the CPS had just disclosed the CRIS (Crime Reporting Information System) report. A CRIS report is a chronological catalogue of how a case is investigated, mine included details such as Gadsby's initial interviews and research, which had taken place before I was served with a notice to attend the station, earlier in the year. Naturally, I was mildly alarmed that the CRIS report had been made available so late in the day. Matt was unsurprised and pointed out that it was pretty obvious the prosecution were playing a game.

His Honour Judge Antony James Leonard QC was presiding over the hearing.

Henry began his argument by summing up the case and the evidence we had so far. He started by stating that the charges against me were important because the complainant had claimed to be fifteen years old, whereas the police knew that he was sixteen at the time.

Henry explained that the charge of indecent assault had

been brought on the basis of the statement of Wasim Anqkar. He told the court that, according to Anqkar, he was arrested by 'Gurpal Virdi and another officer, Tom Makins, and put in the back of a police Sherpa van, where he was physically assaulted by Virdi. During the assault, Virdi inserted his truncheon into Anqkar's anus through his outer clothing.'

Henry then re-emphasised the date of Anqkar's sixteenth birthday – 29 August 1986. The Police National Computer record showed Anqkar was convicted at Balham Juvenile Court on 23 July 1987 in respect of the matter for which he was arrested – that is, possession of an offensive weapon. This highlighted the fact that the police had knowingly released incorrect personal details regarding the complainant to the media, following the summons I'd been issued with earlier that year.

'Anqkar stated that after the incident in the van, Virdi had approached him on a number of occasions and attempted to persuade him to provide information. This was done in such a way as to give the impression to others that Anqkar was a police informer.'

Henry went on to say: 'Anqkar's allegations were made in a recorded interview on 13 March 2013. A witness statement was taken from Anqkar on 1 July 2014; sixteen months after Anqkar was interviewed and after Virdi was summoned.'

This showed the judge that I had been charged before a full investigation into the allegations had been completed.

Henry then turned to the recorded interview with Thomas Makins, who stated that he did not recall seeing Anqkar with

any injuries. Furthermore, in respect of the use of a truncheon, Makins had said that 'he never saw Virdi carrying a
knife, truncheon or any other instruments'.

Henry then turned to Gadsby's investigation into the allegations, highlighting a statement Gadsby had provided about
the extendable baton which 'was not available for shipping to
the UK and that remained the case until after 1987'.

This was important because it directly contradicted what
Anqkar claimed to have seen during the alleged incident – an
ASP, an extendable baton/truncheon.

Henry then outlined relevant case law, highlighting the
fact that a jury would find it difficult to convict anyone based
on the evidence that had been provided so far, and pointing
out the discrepancies associated with it.

Henry said that if the court dismissed the indecent assault
charge, that would leave a single charge of misconduct in
public office. This charge would be based on a combination
of the evidence of Anqkar and Makins to the effect

> that Virdi used excessive force against Anqkar in the van
> by (according to Anqkar) hitting him in the face, holding
> him in a headlock and punching, kicking and kneeing him
> or (according to Makins) wrestling with him and punching
> and possibly kneeing him. These allegations could form a
> charge of common assault, a summary only offence.

This was an important aspect for Henry to point out to the
court, as summary offences can only be brought within a

six-month time period, which did not fit the 28-year gap that we were currently dealing with.

Regarding Makins's testimony, Henry pointed out that if Makins had witnessed an incident then he could have reported this at the time. There was nothing that had prevented him from doing so. But Makins had not reported anything.

'Further, there is no justification for the delay in bringing charges in relation to the assault,' Henry said. 'Given that the incident was witnessed by a serving officer, who failed in his duty to report the commission of a criminal offence committed within his sight and hearing ... the effect in the instant case has been seriously to prejudice Virdi's ability to defend himself.'

In addition, the records relating to the incident were no longer available, a fact which Henry made clear to the court.

'The contemporaneous records, which Virdi would have wished to rely on, are no longer available,' Henry pointed out. 'There is no custody record and neither Virdi's or Makins's notes have been retained. There are no notes in respect of the court appearance at which Anqkar claims he gave evidence. The absence of records is due to the breach of Makins's duty to report the incident.'

In light of all the above, Henry asked the court to dismiss the case.

Julian Evans then stood up on behalf of the Crown.

Evans started by addressing the issue of the ASP that Anqkar claimed I had used when I had assaulted him. But we had already proved to the court that ASPs had not been available to Met officers at the time the alleged incident had taken place.

'On the issue of witness reliability, Anqkar has given an account,' Evans said. 'If he is mistaken as to what that object was, the case should go ahead ... There is no evidence from any other officer, no evidence that police used the ASP at the time, it is a matter for the jury to evaluate.'

Evans turned to the issue of the destroyed evidence.

'The absence of notes is not prejudice to Virdi and is not an abuse of process,' he told the court. 'Serious prejudice has not been identified. Documents are available that Virdi had dealings with Anqkar after October 1986.'

This directly contradicted what Gadsby had stated during my initial interview with him – he claimed five times that all documents had been destroyed and told me court records were only retained for seven years.

'I submit that a fair trial is possible and permissible,' Evans concluded.

Judge Leonard stated that both arguments were well-reasoned and intelligent and he would need some time to deliberate. While we waited for the decision, Sathat and I chatted with Sir Peter Bottomley, while Henry and Matt went off to discuss the finer details of the case.

We had to wait twenty-five minutes before the judge returned to deliver his decision. I had braced myself for bad news and I'd been right to do so. Judge Leonard said that the counts would not be withdrawn and the case would go to trial. We were told to return on 2 October 2014 for further instructions.

I was devastated and everyone in the court was shocked by the judge's decision. Sir Peter Bottomley expressed his anger about the outcome to Matt and Henry, and questioned whether the judge had been in the right court. After saying goodbye, Sir Peter left hurriedly. For me, the judge's verdict had come as no surprise. I felt as if the decision had been made before we had even set foot in the court.

Immediately afterwards, we were served with a new draft indictment. As well as including minor changes, I could see that the two counts had now increased to three:

Indecent Assault (there was no longer an age included)

Misconduct in Public Office

Assault (Actual Bodily Harm ABH)

• • •

After the hearing, Sathat and I had a short meeting with Matt and Henry. We discussed the lack of disclosure and the unfair ruling. There was nothing else we could do at this time.

That evening we went to the Black Police Association (BPA) twentieth anniversary at the Greater London Authority (GLA) building beside the River Thames. In attendance were several people from the community and the police service, and I could sense that people were deliberately ignoring me due to the recent allegations and negative publicity.

Stephen Greenhalgh, Deputy Mayor for Policing and Crime, opened the event, followed by speeches from BPA executives, before Metropolitan Police Commissioner Sir

Bernard Hogan-Howe took to the stage. After he had finished speaking, I stepped up close to the podium to pose some challenging questions. The room fell silent.

Sir Bernard looked at me, but didn't react. He knew I was unafraid of confrontation – especially in matters that involved a miscarriage of justice.

'No questions please,' shouted someone from the crowd.

I asked my first question.

'Commissioner, you talked about equality. Can you say something about what is happening presently – the Carol Howard case? And how the Met is still targeting ethnic minority officers even in retirement?'

'This is not the time or place, Gurpal,' he responded.

'When is the right time?' I pressed him. 'And where is the right place to raise our cases?'

Sir Bernard left the podium. I thought he had taken the coward's way out.

I feel that whenever positive change is promised regarding the Met it's all talk and no action. So far, the government and previous police commissioners have failed in achieving their target of creating a fairer and more equal institution.

The hall fell silent for a few moments. I turned to look at the other guests, some of who were clearly taken aback by my questions, while others carried on as if nothing had happened. People were raising their glasses at me, smiling and quietly saying: 'Well done'; others gave me a thumbs-up sign and silently clapped.

Even though Sir Bernard had left the podium, I continued to ask challenging questions.

'Why does no one want to discuss what is really going on?' I demanded to know. I threw my arms up in disbelief. This was supposed to be the BPA, an organisation that fought against inequality, but it seemed to me they were condoning it. 'Changes will not happen by keeping quiet or being afraid,' I pointed out.

Sathat ran over to me and hurried us back into the crowd. 'What's the matter? Why did you do that?' she said, not particularly pleased with my outburst.

'How else do you fight inequality?' I said. 'This is the only way to go about it – tiptoeing around the situation has given me nothing but grief. I've said it. I feel better now.'

'Then should we head home?'

'No, we'll stay until the dust settles.'

Over the course of the evening, many people came up to me to congratulate me for speaking out. Dr Richard Stone, an anti-racism activist who was involved in the Stephen Lawrence inquiry, was also at the event. I have a great deal of respect for Richard as he did much to expose police mishandling of the Stephen Lawrence case. Now a frail man, he was nevertheless interested in how I was faring, and after I told him about the most recent allegations, he invited me for a meeting. He, too, was disappointed by the other BPA members. They seemed to have lost the will and burning desire to stand up and speak out.

Ben Owusu, a member of the Independent Advisory Group, was less impressed by my behaviour. He said that I had acted out of line towards the commissioner, but he was willing to arrange a meeting with me, so that we could sort things out. After he had expressed his opinions, I responded: 'Really, Ben, come down to earth. This is a long-term fight and I'm thinking of improving things, not just for me, but everyone.'

After the day's events, the failure to get the case dismissed, and the event at the GLA, I continued with my own investigations – I now had a trial to prepare for, and there was much at stake.

I decided to start by reviewing the new documentation we had just received from the CPS. As well as the CRIS report, another document the prosecution had disclosed was Arrest Form 74. This form was used in the 1980s and 1990s by police officers, and would be filled out after making an arrest. During my initial interview, Gadsby had told me that these forms were unavailable as they had been destroyed. Therefore, I felt that not only had Gadsby lied to me, I'd also been asked to undertake a police interview under caution without all the relevant information being made available to me.

Arrest Form 74 details the arrested person's name, address, date and place of birth, sex, height, ethnic appearance, weight, accent, build, voice, eye colour, hair colour/description, marks/scars, dress, occupation, supervising officer, court, crime, crime reference number, date at court, bail conditions and the station involved. A hard copy of the form will then be scanned and saved to the PNC, so that there is a permanent record of every arrest made.

Anqkar's Arrest Form 74 revealed that he had been arrested for the following:

01.03.1987 – Arrest for failing to appear at Balham Juvenile Court. He was charged and kept in custody for court the following day. I was the arresting officer.

23.06.1987 – Arrested for unauthorised taking of a vehicle. He was later charged and found not guilty at Kingston Crown Court. The arresting officer was Police Constable Poole.

26.09.1987 – Arrested for criminal damage to a motor vehicle. He was charged and found guilty at Sutton Magistrates Court. The arresting officer was Sergeant O'Rourke.

23.09.1990 – Arrested for threats to kill and four counts of grievous bodily harm (GBH). After a verbal altercation at a party, he grabbed a female around the neck and threatened to kill her. The report stated that 'her family took exception and deemed to protect her at which Anqkar attacked three of them with a knife stabbing each of them about the body. He was charged and kept in custody. Camberwell Green Magistrates Court discharged the case due to a clerical error.' The arresting officer was Police Constable Roberts.

06.03.1991 – Arrested again for the above as there was further evidence. He was charged. Camberwell Green Magistrates Court again dismissed the case. The arresting officer on this occasion was Detective Constable Hill.

As detailed above, Anqkar had been in trouble with the police on several occasions, although various of the charges were dismissed. However, the only form that interested me was the one pertaining to Anqkar's arrest on 31 October 1986. But this was missing as part of the disclosure. I did notice, however, that I had arrested him for failing to appear at court on 3 March 1987 – so it became apparent that I had had an interaction with Anqkar. But this had been four months after he claimed that I had arrested and assaulted him.

I contacted my friend Jasbir about the latest disclosure. The day after the dismissal hearing, he came over in the afternoon and we went through the documents. The first document that we reviewed was Anqkar's statement.

ANQKAR'S ACCOUNT

After reading the statement, I turned to Jasbir. 'I don't recall any of this,' I said.

'It would be extremely unlikely for a plain-clothes officer to get involved in a dispute between two neighbours,' Jasbir responded. 'Normally incidents like these would be dealt with by uniformed officers.'

I agreed with him. 'In a dispute like the one described, both sides would have been spoken to separately and names would be taken straight away. There's always a reason why a dispute will end in an arrest and in this case it appears to be because Anqkar was carrying a knife,' I commented. 'After an arrest is made, crime squad officers would call in a car and if that wasn't possible they would ask for a station van. So Anqkar's story, that I asked for his name in the back of the van, doesn't quite add up. I would have had plenty of time before the van arrived to ask him for his details. There was no reason for me to attack Anqkar and I highly doubt that handcuffs were used, as there were strict rules surrounding them at the time. If you were to handcuff a suspect, you would have to explain to the custody sergeant why they had been used and provide a serial number.'

'Yes, that's true,' Jasbir responded. 'I remember doing that as a custody officer – we always had to record the reason why someone had been handcuffed on the custody record.'

I explained to Jasbir that the reasons for these strict recording procedures followed on from the Scarman Report recommendations and the introduction of the Police and Criminal Evidence Act (PACE) in 1984.

'I also recall that the van we had was a Ford Transit,' I said.

'You're right, Battersea had the Ford Transit and Lavender Hill had the Sherpa.'

'Furthermore, Anqkar says that he was handcuffed with his hands to his front, after he was placed in the van. This, again, is contradictory to procedure. If a prisoner is violent, then it's best to handcuff him with his hands behind his back. If they're in the front he can still be aggressive and even put an officer in a stranglehold.'

Jasbir agreed: 'I was also always told that when handcuffing a suspect you should always bring their hands behind their back.'

'Exactly,' I said. 'The reason he's claiming that he was handcuffed from the front is because, otherwise, his story of the assault occurring would make no sense and it would be physically impossible to insert an object into his anus. So his account of being handcuffed at the front contradicts police procedure, but helps to make his story plausible.'

Jasbir switched to another aspect of Anqkar's statement: the attempt to open the back doors by kicking them open.

'Doesn't that seem implausible as well?' Jasbir asked.

I agreed. 'At the time of the alleged attack, Battersea were using a Ford Transit, which is the first reason his statement makes no sense,' I said. 'However, let's for argument's sake say they were using a Sherpa. Once either van is locked it's extremely difficult for a prisoner to kick open the doors, as there are metal bars that run from the top to the bottom of the doors. And Anqkar was only 5 foot 6, so it would have been difficult for his legs to even reach the doors. We would always sit the prisoner away from the doors to prevent them from trying to escape.'

Jasbir nodded: 'So he's claiming that the van doors flew open and there were people at the bus stop? Why didn't he shout for help if he was being assaulted? And why didn't Makins mention this in his statement?'

'Exactly,' I said, and then moved to another part of the statement. 'Anqkar also says that I "Mannered" him, and that I was trying to get Anqkar under control. I haven't even heard of "Mannering", I had to look this up. And why would I want to control him?'

'Anqkar states that you wanted him to be an informant,' Jasbir commented.

'Another false accusation,' I said. 'His arrest forms show that he was a low-level criminal, involved in petty crime. Why would he be useful to the Met as an informant? And how does he even know about the whole informant–officer relationship if he's claiming that he's never been in trouble with police before? This informant/money thing is clearly just something he's made up. And it's completely against the rules to go for tea with a juvenile, so why would I ever do it? His statement is just a long list of lies.'

'It certainly looks that way, doesn't it?' Jasbir said.

Then Jasbir turned to the part of the statement where Anqkar claimed that, after taking him to the police station, Tom Makins and I had stood by the cell door 'growling' at him with our 'fists clenched', and Anqkar had then charged towards us.

'I have two questions then,' Jasbir said. 'Firstly, if Anqkar had just been assaulted, how could he have charged towards both you and Tom? He even describes himself, in his statement, as quite nimble and fast at the time. That makes no sense. Secondly, if Anqkar is claiming that Makins was also growling and intimidating, why didn't he raise a complaint against Makins?'

'I have no idea,' I replied. 'That's what makes this so ridiculous. And what's even more ridiculous is Anqkar's claim that I would pick him up, months after the incident, and drive him around. I've never taken a police driving course, didn't have my own car at the time, so the idea of me driving him around in a police car is pure fantasy. I think this is reflective of the extent of lies Anqkar is telling to the police.'

'I also hadn't taken a police driving course in 1986, so completely understand that this is pure fiction. Who has the time to do this anyway when there was so much pressure to investigate offences?'

After reviewing Anqkar's account, we turned to Makins's statement.

MR MAKINS'S ACCOUNT

'The first thing that I noticed', said Jasbir, 'was that Makins's statement doesn't mention the dispute with the neighbour – he says that Anqkar was known to the police. He remembers that there was a fight in the van but that he didn't do anything about it, which I think, if true, clearly shows that he neglected his duties. He also states that Anqkar was uninjured.'

'Yes, he is adamant that Anqkar did not require any form of medical treatment – not even a basic first aid kit.'

I pointed out to Jasbir that Makins had claimed I was prejudiced against West Africans, particularly Nigerians.

'He refers to a specific incident that I was involved in, with a West Indian youth called Geoffrey Mitchell, whereby I had also used excessive force. Now, considering the Met Police gave me a commendation for arresting Mitchell, how can Makins make such an allegation – do they not check the facts?'

'Yes, I can see that,' Jasbir said. 'You would think the investigating police officers would have checked all of this out.'

'Indeed! This is exacerbated by the fact that Makins's testimony confirms that ASPs did not exist at the time, and that he did not remember seeing an ASP until 1989, after transferring to Guernsey. Again, Makins's testimony is in direct contradiction with Anqkar's statement that an ASP was used – how on earth have the CPS proceeded with a case based on such contradictions?'

DWYER'S ACCOUNT

We then turned our attention to a statement made by another police officer, Danny Dwyer, who had worked on the crime squad in Battersea. I had only seen a summary of Dwyer's statement so far, and had been surprised that he was connected to the CPS's case – he was not involved in any of the allegations against me so his part in all this seemed rather out of place.

'He (Dwyer) claims that I had a strong dislike of black people and references an incident where a young black youth spits at both myself and Dwyer and, as a result, I used excessive force by pinning the youth up against a wall,' I told Jasbir. 'It seems like I keep saying this, but if all of this were true, why didn't Dwyer report me at the time? Why is this all coming out in the year 2014, decades after the event?'

'Didn't he go on and work for the Directorate of Professional Standards?' Jasbir said. 'He could have acted then?

In fact, he had the most appropriate platform to report this incident as it related to your professional performance.'

I looked Jasbir in the eye.

'Well, we know why, don't we? You can't report an incident that never happened. Again, Dwyer confirms that ASPs would not have been available at the time of the alleged incident. That's the second police officer to directly contradict Anqkar's account.'

ZINZAN'S ACCOUNT

The fourth and final statement we examined was that made by David Zinzan. I'd known him from Battersea as he had joined two months after me, and I'd had a good relationship with him.

'His statement describes you as being confrontational and having a particularly negative attitude towards Africans,' Jasbir commented. 'He obviously hasn't heard about your work with the Black Police Association.'

'No, I guess not,' I replied. 'He states that he is absolutely clear that he did not use ASPs at the time, and that he never saw one all of the times he was in Battersea. In fact, he actually states 1997 as the first time he was issued with one,' I pointed out. 'To be honest, I'm really disappointed in Zinzan. I really thought he was a decent guy – he even came to my wedding and has come over to my house before. While I was based at New Scotland Yard, he was briefly my boss and we'd have lunch and discuss the old times at Battersea. He told me about how his son was sick. None of it makes sense. Why would a senior officer, who genuinely believed that I was racist, go for lunch with me and pay for the meal?'

'All of this seems bizarre,' Jasbir said. 'Didn't Zinzan work on the unsolved Daniel Morgan murder case and work for the DPS?'

I nodded.

'Why didn't he mention any of this earlier?' Jasbir asked. 'I see a common theme here,' Jasbir continued. 'All three police officers have essentially said the same things, but in various ways. Firstly, you have a negative attitude towards black people. They all corroborate this with an unreported, random example that appears not to have been verified as part of the police investigation. Secondly, they all state that ASPs were unavailable and not used in 1986, or in fact for many years after – all direct contradictions to Anqkar's statement. The one guy, Makins, who claims to be there, didn't even see a sexual assault. How this case has even made it past CPS's desk is beyond me.'

'Even if any of this were true, after leaving Battersea, I joined the SO11 Squad, which dealt with surveillance and intelligence,' I pointed out. 'We were rigorously screened during the selection process given the nature of the work we would be doing, and therefore if I was a violent person and prejudiced towards people from different backgrounds, I think my application would have been rejected, don't you?'

After a few minutes reflecting on our analysis of the

statements, we decided to call it a day. We had got a lot done, had started to identify common themes that would help the defence. As Jasbir was quite ill, I left him to rest.

Following the failure of our dismissal of the allegations earlier in the week, I headed back to Southwark Crown Court to be formally charged. I had woken up that morning to read the following headline in the *Daily Mirror*: 'Former detective accused of sexually assaulting teenage boy with his truncheon'.

It was becoming a pattern that before each court hearing headlines referring to my case and the allegations would appear in the press. As I wasn't speaking to any newspaper reporters, it followed that the Met was continuing to issue press releases, intent on destroying me and my credibility.

I was asked to enter a plea against the charges put to me, and I pleaded not guilty. A trial date was then set for 27 July 2015, with Judge Leonard presiding. I was granted un-conditional bail. I left the court feeling deflated and was in desperate need of some cheering up, so I met up for lunch with Kesar, who worked nearby.

'So what happened at court?' Kesar asked.

'Nothing much, it was just a formality,' I answered. 'I was charged and I pleaded not guilty. The date of the trial has been fixed for next July – it'll be the same judge.'

'What do you think are the chances of winning your case? Is it up to the judge?'

'No, the case doesn't depend on him. It'll be the jury that decides.'

'If I was on the jury, and I had heard about the hell you have been put through, in addition to the complete lack of credible evidence, I would throw the case out.'

'That's because you know me,' I told her. 'Members of the jury will look at the facts and be guided to the evidence by the judge. Anyway, it's different now. This time I can talk to you, Kushal and Tasvir about the case. The last time this happened you were all so young – your mum and I kept a lot of things from you in order to protect you.'

'We're all here for you and will do whatever we can to help. You know that, right?'

'I know. I've been going through the documents at home and some will definitely be useful. You're all always accusing me of hoarding, but now you can see I am cautious for a reason.'

'I have to agree with Mum, you do hoard a lot of documents. You should try taking up a hobby that keeps you out of trouble – why don't you get a dog? You know you want one.'

'Looking after a dog is hard work, sadly they don't live that long.'

I was glad that I had the support from the children. I knew the coming months would be very difficult, and having such reassurance did a lot to help.

CHAPTER 12

DEEP DIVE

With the court date set, Matt and I had just over ten months to provide enough evidence to a jury to show that the allegations were completely false. We collated all the documentation we had received and began our own enquiries into potential witnesses.

The first names on our list were those of Graham Markwick and Paul Mady.

Detective Constable Graham Markwick was important because his name appeared on a conviction certificate we had received from the CPS. This certificate, produced by the court, showed Anqkar's sentence in relation to the incident of 31 October 1986, when he was arrested for carrying an offensive weapon and a breach of the peace.

It is important to note that each conviction certificate names the arresting officer: the certificate produced by the court named Graham Markwick as the man who had arrested Anqkar. It follows, then, that I could not have assaulted Anqkar on 31 October 1986, as I had not been the arresting officer. But why had Gadsby failed to interview the only person directly linked to Anqkar's arrest? My name was not on the certificate, yet I stood accused of arresting and assaulting Anqkar.

Paul Mady had been my partner on the crime squad in Battersea. This was why it seemed highly unusual for Makins to have stated that the two of us had been partners at the time of the alleged incident. Matt and I decided we needed to contact Paul to confirm that he had, indeed, been my partner at the time.

Tracking down Paul was fairly easy; I did an internet search, established that he ran a football club and took it from there. On Friday 3 October, Matt and I drove to Surrey to speak with Paul. My ex-colleague now lived in a clean, quiet residential street with semi-detached houses. I knocked on the door but got no answer, so I tried a few neighbouring houses. But no one was at home.

'Shall I call him on his mobile, Matt?'

'No, leave it. I'll put a note through the letterbox.' Matt took a piece of paper from his bag and started writing. 'If you call him then it might be perceived as interfering with witnesses.'

'But he isn't a witness,' I pointed out.

'We can't be certain of that. Maybe the Met have spoken to him and have managed to ascertain a statement already, but failed to inform us.'

'It's disgusting that they are allowed to behave like this,' I said.

'Yeah, but they can get away with it,' Matt responded.

After leaving a note in Paul's letterbox, Matt and I then

travelled to Graham Markwick's house. But, as had happened at Paul's home, we got no answer when we knocked
on the door. I began to worry that the entire trip was going to
prove fruitless.

Then, thankfully, Graham appeared at a side door. He was
dressed for gardening and his hands were covered in soil, but
although he was older now, I still recognised him. We stared
at each other for a few seconds, before I said: 'Hello Graham,
how are you?'

'Oh my God, George! How are you, my old friend?'

Graham came forward and we hugged and he kissed me
on the cheek.

'Don't worry, I won't try and kiss you too,' he told Matt.
Graham had always been a bit of a joker – he made some leg-
endary Christmas speeches during which he always poked
fun at senior management.

Graham took us into the kitchen and busied himself
making tea. I started to explain why Matt and I were visiting
him, but Graham halted me mid-sentence.

'George, I have read about it, don't worry,' he said.

I looked at him with gratitude and then explained that
Matt needed to speak with him privately. A couple of minutes
later, Lesley, Graham's wife, arrived home with the shopping.
She recognised me immediately and we exchanged pleasant-
ries. It had been twenty years, yet she still remembered me.

Matt and Graham went to another room to chat, while I
stayed with Lesley in the kitchen. I was worried that if I was
in the same room as Matt and Graham while they discussed

the evidence the Met would accuse me of trying to influence a witness. At this point we were unsure whether Graham or Paul had been approached by the Met.

Lesley and I retreated to the garden and I told her the reason for my impromptu visit. She was shocked but not entirely surprised. Lesley understood the politics of the Met, having worked as a PA to a very senior officer. We had a nice catch-up, reminiscing about old times, as we waited for Matt and Graham to finish their chat.

After a while, Graham and Matt joined us in the garden. As Graham and Lesley were going out, we were unable to take a formal statement, so we set off home. I was dying to quiz Matt about the details of his conversation with Graham, and whether anything he'd said would be helpful for our defence. But I did not want to compromise his position.

After we had arrived at my home, Matt told me that he had received further disclosure from the CPS, which included Anqkar's police interview video. I pulled out my laptop and we watched the video together. As I watched, I tried my hardest to place Anqkar, but I could not recognise him at all. I felt angry that this man was making such vile accusations against me – I felt sick to my stomach watching the video.

Matt and I had a lengthy discussion about what we had just seen. We both thought there were significant gaps in Anqkar's version of events, which contradicted the written statements we had received. Anqkar also came across as being insincere. As it was getting late, we decided to call it a day there. I dropped Matt off at a bus stop and he made his way home.

Later that evening, Matt texted me to say he would try and meet Paul Mady the next day. At the same time, I received a message from Paul. I'd been reluctant to return his call as I was worried it would be seen as me interfering with a witness.

A couple of days later, Matt met with Paul and, thankfully, their meeting went well. Matt managed to obtain a statement; he was still working on getting one from Graham.

A week later, Sathat and I went to meet Dr Richard Stone in Finchley. An anti-racism activist, Dr Stone was awarded an OBE for services to the public and voluntary services in 2010. His father, Lord Stone, was a Labour peer and his uncle Lord Ashdown had sat on the Conservative benches in the House of Lords. But, despite his family's political connections, Richard became a campaigner by chance while working as a GP in Westminster. He is perhaps best known for his involvement in the inquiry into the 1993 murder of Stephen Lawrence, an inquiry I have always strongly supported. Richard worked closely with the Lawrence family and spent a great deal of time with officers, which allowed him to gain an idea of who he could trust.

Richard listened attentively as I told him about my case and, although there was little he could do, he said that he was willing to speak to Matt.

'The evidence you gave to the Stephen Lawrence inquiry

was invaluable, and it confirmed what we as panel members suspected was going on,' said Richard.

'At the time, I was ostracised and threatened by senior officers for my involvement,' I responded. 'But I knew I had done the right thing and that the truth needed to come out.'

Reflecting back on the Stephen Lawrence case, I told Richard that I thought that it was unbelievable that officers, who were all fully trained first-aiders, were denying that they had any first aid knowledge.

'The other thing that got me was senior officers claiming that they didn't know their powers of arrest, yet they were sitting on promotion boards,' I added.

'Gurpal has always been a very conscientious officer. He's always given his time and been involved in community groups,' Sathat interjected.

'Personally, I get great satisfaction from helping people who are in trouble through no fault of their own,' Richard responded.

He then invited us to his study to show us his book. When he learnt that Sathat worked in a library, he gave us two signed copies: one for us and the second as a donation to the library.

About a week later, I met Matt again to discuss the case and to check if he'd made any progress. Graham had still not made a statement and Matt had been unable to pay a visit to Richard.

I had spent the past week going through all my paperwork, and had discovered that Tom Makins had never been my partner, and that Makins was wrong about that. Back then I had had only two permanent police partners: Paul Mady and Derek True.

Matt was perplexed. He didn't understand why Makins could make the statement he had made or why he would choose to testify against me. I still couldn't help but think that Makins was perhaps confusing me with another Asian officer he had worked with in the same area. Matt agreed this was possible, but added that it would be a problematic line of argument to pursue as both Anqkar and Makins had placed me in the van where the alleged assault had taken place.

We decided to go through Michael Doherty's phone recording and Anqkar's interview video again – perhaps we were missing something. But we failed to find any further helpful information.

We then focused on the CRIS report that we'd received. These reports chronologically detailed the investigation of the alleged crime Anqkar had reported, including all interactions with witnesses. It was very long, about 115 pages. This was an important part of our investigation, as it would not only provide an understanding of the investigation, but would also perhaps show how and where important details may have been missed.

We sat at the table, side by side, with the report between us.

'So, the investigation was initially conducted by the Sapphire team in 2013,' I said. 'If you turn to p. 40, you'll see that on 6 March DC Hastings writes that the victim was fourteen to fifteen years old in 1985 – which means that he was sixteen/ seventeen years old in 1986 and twenty-six to twenty-seven in 1997. Anqkar's age was clearly correctly confirmed at a very early stage of the investigation by the Sapphire team, but for some reason Gadsby kept claiming during my police interview that he was fifteen in 1986.

'On p. 50 we can see that, on 14 March 2013, DC Hastings requested assistance from the DPS Intelligence to help identify the Asian officer that Anqkar refers to. It was requested for: "an Asian male police officer working in Battersea 1985 known by the nickname of 'George' and believed to be called 'Virdi Girdi'."

'And, within a few minutes, the DPS had named me, confirming my name, that I was stationed at Battersea from 1982 and known to his colleagues as "George".

'Then Hastings provided the DPS with a crime reference number for Anqkar's arrest – C2588/87. This was because it linked my name directly with Anqkar. The "C" signals that it is a criminal matter. However, crucially, this crime that links me took place in 1987 and not 1986, the year Anqkar claims. So they are associating me with the wrong criminal matter.

'The CRIS report showed that senior officers then discussed who would lead the investigation, despite it having been established that I was only involved with Anqkar in 1987.'

We then studied the report that showed that, on 9 May 2013, DC Hastings had received Anqkar's conviction certificate for possession of an offensive weapon in 1986. The certificate clearly showed Anqkar's date of birth was given as

29 August 1970, and that the arresting officer in the case was DC Markwick.

DC Hastings then tried to ascertain the identity of Markwick. But, instead of providing the DPS with Markwick's unique staff code (a warrant number), Hastings provided the DPS with the crime number shown on the conviction certificate. The DPS replied with the following: 'the informant is listed as DC Markwick W/No 5347/86 – a female officer who with such a low warrant number has clearly retired.'

I looked at Matt.

'What on earth is going on?' I said. 'They have obviously confused the crime number that is shown on the conviction certificate as Markwick's staff code. This means they have mistaken Markwick as a woman. Their investigation into Markwick stops here. This is incompetence at its highest – they cannot establish that Graham Markwick is a man who served with me in Battersea.'

Matt's shock was obvious as the flaws of the investigation became apparent to him. We then turned to p. 70, which concerned DC Hastings officially handing over the case from the Sapphire team to the DPS on 16 July 2013.

Matt asked why the case had been passed to DPS and not continued by Sapphire.

'Under normal circumstances, this would have stayed with Sapphire,' I answered. 'I don't know why this was passed on to DPS – I have my suspicions, but let's not go into that right now.'

Matt gave me a knowing look.

The report showed that the DPS passed the case to DC Gadsby on 17 July 2013. The handover to Gadsby included the conviction certificate dated 1987, relating to the incident for possession of an offensive weapon in 1986. It is important to reiterate that DC Gadsby and his team must have known that Anqkar was sixteen years old when he was convicted.

DI Donna Smith became the supervising caseworker, while DC Gadsby was appointed investigating officer and DCI Fiona McCormack was named senior investigating officer. The CRIS report showed that, after reviewing the case file, DI Smith was unconvinced by Anqkar's story.

The report also stated that 'the victim was convicted for carrying an offensive weapon (namely a lock knife).'

Matt and I noted that DI Smith had confirmed that the actual conviction was for a lock knife, and not the Stanley knife that Anqkar had claimed in both his written statement and police interview.

DI Smith went on to state: 'DC Markwick is shown as the OIC and has been identified through enquiries as Graham Markwick (now retired).'

'So, Matt,' I explained. 'An OIC is the officer in case, usually the arresting officer, and it looks like they have finally determined that Markwick is a man and not a retired woman.' Matt laughed.

DI Smith then stated: 'The main witness is "Tom". Enquiries are currently underway to identify "Tom", at which point an approach will be made.'

'It looks like the line of investigation into Markwick has stopped, for some bizarre reason, and then Tom Makins is all of a sudden named as a main witness,' I told Matt. 'However, his name isn't on any of the official police documents, nor the court documents pertaining to Anqkar's charges; we only have his written statement'.

The CRIS report then corroborated Ben Owusu's claims that a Gold Group had been set up, due to the reputational and organisational risks involved with the case. Following this, DC Gadsby moved the restriction level of the case up to 'confidential' and named the operation 'Gianna', a female given name that translates from Italian as 'God is gracious'.

'Do you think giving the operation an Italian name has something to do with your surname?' Matt queried. 'You know, after Verdi the composer?'

'I think it's what they do for ethnic minority officers,' I said. 'When they were investigating Ali Dizaei, all of us were given Italian names.'

We were making progress, but I knew it was important for us to keep going through the report with a fine-tooth comb, so we continued.

'So the report states that DC Gadsby decided to speak to a colleague about the crime squad in Battersea and was pointed in the direction of Danny Dwyer, who had worked for DPS but had been posted to Battersea in the '80s. Dwyer was now teaching at a police training school, following thirty years of service.'

Matt chimed in and said the report showed that Dwyer recalled having worked with me, but that Dwyer did not recall a 'Tom'. According to the report, Dwyer had suggested that Gadsby contact David Zinzan, who had also worked in Battersea. He had later worked for the DPS, and was now Deputy Chief Constable of Devon and Cornwall.

The report showed that, with the assistance of Zinzan, Gadsby had managed to confirm that 'Tom' was actually Thomas Makins, who had left the Met in May 1987 and joined the police in Guernsey. Despite living and working in Guernsey, Tom would still attend Battersea reunions and Zinzan had last seen him about a year ago.

'Matt, I haven't been invited to a single one of these reunions, just so that you know.'

Matt wanted to know more about the reunions, so I explained.

'Most stations in the Met have reunions,' I said. 'Back in the old days they would be publicised and everyone would be welcome, but they've become quite exclusive. It's very much if you are not part of the group, you're not invited.'

'I see,' said Matt.

'Anyway, so Gadsby spoke to Dwyer again and invited him to be part of the inquiry,' I said. 'Dwyer had promised he would supply a statement for the police, but he also said that I wouldn't have been carrying an ASP, and that ASPs weren't issued until the mid-'90s.'

Matt then pointed to comments that had been made by Gadsby, which read as follows:

One of the aspects of Mr Anqkar's account I find a little strange is his description of the object implemented into his anus. Mr Anqkar ... would seem to be describing an ASP. I believe that ASPs were not issued to MPS personnel in 1986 ... If Mr Anqkar is making up this allegation he may not have realised that ASPs were not in common usage in the '80s and has only described this as this is an item he has seen police officers with in recent years.

I nodded: 'Oh, yes, I see. So Gadsby also appears to be unconvinced but obviously presses on.'

Gadsby had visited Anqkar to probe him on this issue and had then stated in the report:

Mr Anqkar provides a very compelling account which is consistent and accurate when probed. The ASP issue is answered in that Mr Anqkar states that after the attack, during the times Mr Virdi was harassing him, he saw the ASP and saw Mr Virdi flicking it out and demonstrating how it happened.

I thought for a minute. 'So, perhaps one of the most important aspects of this case – the ASP that I allegedly used to assault Anqkar – Gadsby has deemed to be a minor mistake on Anqkar's part, which was then later explained. This makes no sense – there was no bloody ASP, yet Gadsby is still pursuing this!'

'Is it usual for police officers to note that it is a very compelling account which is consistent and accurate?' Matt asked.

'No, because you have only heard one side of the story,' I answered. 'It would seem that DC Gadsby may already have made his mind up on how to proceed with the investigation.'

'Let's continue,' I said. 'On 22 July 2013, the officers involved – Stevens, McCormack, Smith and Gadsby – decide to treat "Tom" as a significant witness. The DPS informed the Gold Group and the IPCC of this progression. The IPCC is supposed to be an independent body yet they are fully aware of the investigation – where is the independence in this?'

'A significant witness is someone who claims to have witnessed, visually or otherwise, an indictable offence including serious physical assault and sexual assault,' Matt clarified. 'It appears that this is how DPS are utilising Tom Makins.'

'Yes, and here, look, at p. 79 – on 29 July 2013, DC Gadsby and DI Donna Smith travelled to Guernsey to conduct an interview with Makins,' I said. 'This interview was recorded on an audio device. It is almost the same as the written statement he (Makins) has provided confirming that I used excessive force on Anqkar in a police van. He also threw another name into the mix, stating that the van was being driven by a Dave Wilberforce or Wildbore.'

Matt pointed out that both Gadsby and Smith had tried to extract more information about the incident. Firstly, they focused on the claim of 'excessive force'. But Makins was unable to explain what he had meant by using the phrase. Matt elaborated: 'Furthermore, Makins corroborates yours and everyone else's assertion that ASPs were not around in the 1980s, and that the first time he had seen one was years later when he was serving in Guernsey.'

'So Makins doesn't see an ASP, Anqkar gets it wrong and on both counts, Gadsby insists that an ASP was used as per the original charges. Furthermore, why have they completely failed to find the Dave Wilberforce/Wildbore character that Makins references – surely that is an obvious witness to pursue in this investigation?'

Matt looked at me. 'Makins seems to think that he has seen you use excessive force at other times,' Matt said. 'He tells Gadsby and Smith that you used excessive force involving Geoffrey Mitchell. That this happened on York Road, Battersea, but he could not recall when this happened and was rather non-committal about the circumstances.'

'This never happened. This is yet another lie,' I said. 'I have no idea why he's saying all of this. The reports show that Gadsby makes enquiries on the police national computer and to prisons to track down Geoffrey Mitchell.'

The CRIS report showed that, on 8 August 2013, the Gold Group met, and the following points were recorded:

- ASPs were not issued to police at the time of offence. In 1998, Virdi's home address was searched for 7 hours by PolSA anti-terrorist team, in relation to another matter. No ASP was found or noted on this search.

- Whilst Virdi was serving in the MPS, it has been recorded that he was a victim of racism on more than one occasion.
- There are pictures of Virdi on the internet as recent as last year.
- The victim is aware via a third party that the suspect (Virdi) has been in the press.
- Re: Tom Makins: account is very vague and non-committal; senior officer to approach him. Provide assurances and request further assistance. Makins to be visited again.
- Police to contact Deputy Chief Constable David Zinzan.
- Police to re-visit Makins (NB: this was not done; Zinzan spoke to Makins).
- Further enquiries to be made re: the ASP.

'The Gold Group explicitly point out that their significant witness, Makins, provides an account that is very vague and non-committal,' Matt said. 'I still don't understand why on earth the CPS progressed this.'

I pointed out: 'The report states that following the Gold Group session and Makins's account … Gadsby was tasked to contact Zinzan as it was deemed necessary to discuss matters in relation to a possible further approach to Makins. Makins's statement was sent to Zinzan. Gadsby also makes enquiries on the PNC and prisons to track down Geoffrey Mitchell, the other black male mentioned by Makins.

'Zinzan's role is clearly questionable as he is a witness against you and also assisting the investigating team to put pressure on Makins,' said Matt.

We continued examining the reports and stopped at entries made in September 2013.

'It says that contact is made with Geoffrey Mitchell by Gadsby, initially by phone, but then meets him with DS Ryan,' I said. 'Mitchell tells Gadsby that, back in the '80s, he was a bit of a rogue and a "bit of a lad". He recalls me as being on his back all the time, but could not recall any incidents when he was assaulted by a police officer.'

'So you remember this Geoffrey Mitchell guy then?' Matt enquired.

'Yes, I do remember – he sticks out in my memory, but only because the Met Police gave me a commendation for his arrest.'

'Geoffrey also confirms that the crime squad in Battersea were doing their job and cannot remember them being overtly violent. This directly contradicts Anqkar's account again.'

As Makins had referred specifically to Mitchell, the report showed that Gadsby had spent time trying to connect Makins and Mitchell to a specific incident. He had done so by reviewing Mitchell's criminal convictions, mainly for theft and drugs, from 1985 to 1989. There was one instance in 1989, when Mitchell had been convicted for possessing an offensive weapon, drugs, criminal damage and assaulting a police constable. Gadsby tried to link this conviction with what Makins had told him, but the problem was that Mitchell's conviction had been in 1989 and Makins had left Battersea in 1987.

After reading this, Matt said: 'So, there is no evidence link-
ing Makins to Mitchell – so when did he witness this supposed
attack, when you supposedly used excessive force against
Mitchell? Which Mitchell himself claims never happened!'

'I'm not sure,' I said. 'The whole thing is madness and the
lines of enquiry just make no sense. Even Mitchell claims he
never saw the crime squad carry an ASP.'

I continued: 'Gadsby himself states that his meeting with
Mr Mitchell was "somewhat disappointing". He clearly didn't
get the corroborating story from Mitchell that he needed.
The fact that Makins names him, and Gadsby fails to get a
statement just because the meeting was disappointing, does
not sound like a proper police investigation.'

'Look here,' said Matt, 'look at what Zinzan emails to
Gadsby in October 2013.'

I immediately read what Matt had just alerted me to. In his
email to Gadsby, Zinzan had written:

> I telephoned Tom Makins today … after exchanging
> pleasantries I got on to the subject of the Battersea crime
> squad and then the incident that took place in the rear of
> the police van … he was adamant he had nothing further
> to add … he is very clear he saw no ASP or any other im-
> plement of a similar design.

Gadsby then goes on to write that Zinzan was able to provide
me with a contact telephone number for Jim Warnock: 'Mr
Warnock was apparently Mr Virdi's partner in 1986–87. I'm

somewhat reluctant to contact Mr Warnock as I do not know what if any relationship still exists between them.'

'So, there are a few significant things in this passage, Gurpal,' Matt said. 'Firstly, Zinzan once again is taking an active role in this investigation, when he is also a witness against you. Secondly, why isn't there any documentation to show follow-up with Mr Warnock? This is the second person, after Mady, that was your partner during the time of the alleged incident, but was not spoken to. Makins, who was never your partner, is somehow their key witness. Lastly, there is no ASP – again!'

'Yes, this is just one more example of how not to conduct a police investigation,' I said. 'It's like the bloopers! These are obvious key lines of enquiry, which have not been followed – stuff that is taught to you in Hendon!'

We went on to examine the minutes from a subsequent Gold Group meeting held on 10 October 2013. We underlined the following notes from the minutes as we thought they were the most relevant:

- The ASP has never been seen by anyone and cannot therefore be corroborated.
- Enquiries continue to identify the van driver, although a possibility is Dave Wilberforce.
- There is nothing in Virdi's history file re: any assaults.

Despite the obvious flaws in the investigation thus far, the reports stated that Gadsby had passed the case file to the

CPS on 29 October 2013. This was for the CPS to review, and to provide initial comments and guidance regarding the direction of the investigation. The case was assigned to a Mr Andrew Levin. The CRIS report showed that four months after the case file was submitted to the CPS, Levin went back to Gadsby and asked for a question to be put to Makins concerning the use of torches.

It is important to note that all discussions and meetings in relation to this case that took place at Gold Group meetings were not shown to Andrew Levin from the Crown Prosecution Service, prior to him authorising the charges in April 2014.

I exchanged looks with Matt. 'This feels rather desperate. They have ascertained that ASPs do not exist and would not have been used during an assault, so now are trying to come up with alternatives to make Anqkar's story plausible.'

Gadsby went on to state in the CRIS report:

I have now met with Mr Levin, CPS, and discussed the case with him. Whilst he was not willing to commit himself at this stage with regards to a decision on charging he did state that the issues with the ASP, whilst harming the prosecution case, in his opinion would not fatally harm the case.

'So, CPS acknowledge that the prosecution case is weak?' Matt said.

'Yes, Gadsby goes on to state that Levin would not be able to consider the investigation until my account of what happened had been gained.'

In March 2014, after nearly a year of initial investigations, Gadsby wrote the following: 'Following the Gold Group last week a decision has been made to speak to Mr Virdi. It is intended to do this from a caution … if he decides he does not wish to come with us he will be arrested.'

CHAPTER 13

TYING UP
LOOSE ENDS

As a family we were trying to be 'normal', but the impact of the allegations and the impending trial were taking their toll. Sathat's health wasn't brilliant, but she continued to be a source of strength. I threw myself into council casework and did my utmost to help the local residents.

My role as a councillor brought some relief and allowed me to attend significant events, such as my first Remembrance Sunday service in Cranford as a councillor. Other councillors were also in attendance and it was lovely to see people from different political backgrounds united in honouring those who had lost their lives during the war. I distinctly remember seeing a little girl standing with her mother, who looked eager to get involved. All councillors are required to lay a wreath, so I turned to the little girl's mother and asked if her daughter would like to lay the wreath with me. Together, we then laid it on behalf of the mayor. After the ceremony, the girl's mother thanked me for affording her daughter such an honour. 'It is the only way they learn and respect those who have died for the country,' I responded.

• • •

It was Sathat's birthday in November so we decided to go away for a few days to celebrate. We agreed that Berlin would be the perfect place to visit, as neither of us had ever been before. It was a truly beautiful city, steeped in history, but most importantly the time away from London allowed us to relax and think about things other than the case.

December rolled in and the festive season was upon us, which brought with it a myriad of events – family gatherings and councillor functions. Sadly, I was subdued and not in the mood to socialise – I was hurt by the bad publicity I was receiving and during these dark days I became somewhat of a recluse.

Despite feeling low, there were functions that I was still eager to make the effort to attend. One such event was held at the Indian High Commission to mark the tragedy of the First World War. Following the Second World War, many people living in the Commonwealth chose to emigrate to the UK. Some of these new immigrants applied to join the police force, yet they were rejected on the basis of their skin colour. I found this ironic, as during the war so many Asian members of the Commonwealth had volunteered to fight alongside British soldiers and ultimately gave up their lives to protect Britain. It is worth noting that Britain was willing to put ethnic minority Commonwealth volunteers on the front line, yet were unwilling to allow them to join the police force. What hypocrisy!

Christmas was upon us and there were suddenly presents to buy, a tree to put up and decorate, and guests to welcome to the house. I also had local church events to attend and I needed to check up on the elderly living in our area to make sure they were OK. It was safe to say that I had a lot to keep me busy.

As the New Year came about, my health took a turn for the worse. The stress of the trial continued to adversely impact me and my ears became permanently blocked. I was prescribed medication by my GP, but it didn't seem to be working. My ears bled so much one night that I ended up in hospital, where I received urgent treatment and medication. Eventually the doctors discovered I had blocked sinuses, which explained the dizzy spells I'd been experiencing. I would need to undergo an operation, but I wanted to wait until after the trial, so they put me on medication and gave me a strong nasal spray.

At a council meeting in January, councillors were informed by the chief executive of Hounslow Council that their head of legal services, Richard Gruet, would be seeking early retirement and would leave with a full pension.

To give this some context, in the autumn of the previous year, I had written to the Metropolitan Police Commissioner to ask about the status of ethnic minority officers in Hounslow – this enquiry rose out of some casework I was conducting in Hounslow. The letter was passed to local borough Chief Superintendent Carl Bussey. I then received emails from Bussey's staff officer, who asked me to make an FoI request for the information. But I refused. It seemed counter-productive to do so, as most of the data I required could only be provided by the central human resources department of the Metropolitan Police.

A month later, I received an email from Richard Gruet re-garding the letter I'd sent to the commissioner. Gruet stated that he was considering reprimanding me for breaching council rules, as I had used the wrong type of letterhead when making my request. To me this seemed petty – had I actually just received an email from the head of legal services for using the wrong letterhead paper? The whole thing was bizarre.

I responded by asking Gruet how he knew about my letter to the commissioner. He replied that he had been made aware by Mary Harpley, the council's chief executive, so I decided to email Mary to get to the bottom of the matter. In my email, I explained that my request had been passed to the council's administration team, who had then printed and sent my letter to the commissioner. Any problems regarding letter-heads or printing would not have been my responsibility.

I followed this up with another email to both Harpley and Gruet, asking who had informed them of my information re-quest. I received an apology from Gruet, explaining that it had been Bussey who had approached Mary about my request. The whole thing was strange. I had put in an information request and it had ended with the head of legal services threatening me with disciplinary action for using the wrong letterhead paper. It seemed as if people were desperate to see me fail and were accusing me of things that I hadn't been responsible for.

In February, Matt received further disclosure from the CPS. It wasn't the full disclosure that we were still waiting for, but it was helpful information in building our case against Anqkar. The disclosure related to a case that dated back to 2006 and which involved Anqkar. After reading the document, I called Matt to discuss it.

'This document is a report that shows corruption charges relating to staff at a council housing office. Anqkar was breeding dogs, which he would then exchange for parking permits or would sell the puppies. Even the local MP deemed it so serious that she got the police involved. Did you read where Anqkar is getting one of the witnesses to sign a typed statement while wearing rubber gloves?' I said.

'Yes. He clearly knows about forensics and the consequences of his actions. The CPS have said the prosecution will strongly resist efforts to introduce the corruption charges in the trial,' Matt responded.

'Yet Gadsby still wants to portray him as a victim in allegations against me. Anqkar was charged with corruption and perverting the course of justice, although the charges were not proceeded with. This cannot be right.'

'Gurpal, I understand your frustration, but we have to fight this in a calm manner.'

We ended the call there.

• • •

During spring, council duties had kept me busy, but I was starting to get distracted by the upcoming case again. At public events, gatherings and meetings, people kept asking me questions about the police targeting me. Most people in the community were aware of my background, my history with the police and my knowledge of the law. As a result, I received several calls from people asking for advice. One local resident had received a summons and wanted to know what to do next, so he gave me a ring. People tend to panic when they receive legal or police documents and the first person they choose to get in touch with in Hounslow is usually me – I don't charge for my advice and guidance.

In a similar vein, I tried to reach out to people with influence who could possibly help me. In March, I phoned Simon Woolley, director of Operation Black Vote, an organisation that aims to increase political education and promote equality and human rights. I asked him if he would meet me to discuss my case. He said that he had read articles about me but said he wanted to talk to Lee Jasper, a former senior policy advisor on equalities to the London Mayor, before arranging a meeting. He never called me back. This is the reality of what I was facing. People who possessed the influence to support me washed their hands of me – it was becoming a common theme.

By the time May came along, we had still received no further disclosure from the CPS. The trial was now only a couple of months away, so I called Matt to ask if he had received any updates on when we might get disclosure.

Matt confirmed that the prosecution had not yet provided

full disclosure, so he would have to make a court application to request it. It was clear that the prosecution were not abiding by court instructions and that Matt would have to escalate the matter. This would mean paying more fees and that we would have to continue building our case without all of the information that should have been made available to us. It was frustrating. It felt as if there was no further evidence supporting the prosecution's case to be released, so the Met and the CPS were trying to bide their time and find new evidence that would benefit them.

In the meantime, I continued with my own investigations. This included making enquiries about Samantha Fletcher, whom Anqkar named in his police interview. He claimed that she had worked as a social worker at the youth club he used to visit with Denzel as a teenager.

I checked with the British Association of Social Workers, and received the following response: 'We are unable to give out personal information, but I can tell you that person has never been registered with us.'

Again, this might cast doubt on Anqkar's testimony – did Fletcher exist and, if so, had she ever been a social worker?

I wanted an official position on the issue of ASPs. We had already determined via various statements that officers in the UK did not carry ASPs in the 1980s. I asked Sir Peter Bottomley MP if he could confirm from the Home Office when ASPs were first issued. The Home Office replied: 'The Metropolitan Police Service first had authorisation to use a collapsible baton on 28 June 1995.'

On 3 June, Matt and I were called to Henry's chambers to discuss the case. Henry told us the prosecution had emailed him to say that Anqkar's fingerprints had been taken and documented by me after the arrest.

Matt's initial question was: 'Which arrest are they referring to?'

'They didn't say,' responded Henry.

'Well, in that case, we need more information,' I added. 'Particularly the dates on which the fingerprints were taken and other details that would normally be recorded on fingerprint forms like name, DOB and crime reference number.'

'I'll go back and ask,' Henry said. He looked concerned, but I knew that if the documents were going to cause a problem, they would have been produced at the beginning of the trial. But I felt there was something off about the timing of the new evidence.

'Henry, Gurpal, we have still not received the CRB check that triggered Anqkar to report the allegations. The prosecution still haven't provided it as of yet.' Matt reminded us.

We were still asking for important disclosure regarding this case. Since I had been charged, Matt had had to send several letters to the CPS, even threatening to list the case for non-disclosure. We were asking for important documents that were vital to my case but were not forthcoming.

Still angry at the prosecution's attempts to throw in unreliable evidence at such a late stage, I was spurred on when I returned home that evening to find new information to discredit Anqkar.

When investigating suspects, police officers will often look up names in the bankruptcy and insolvency register. After typing in Anqkar's name, an interesting search result caught my eye: Anqkar had apparently become bankrupt as a result of deception, but had failed to appear in court for the offence. This was the first time that there was a potential financial motive to Anqkar's claims. A few days later, I received the registered copy of Anqkar's marriage certificate to Leah Caraboo. I now had in my possession a tangible piece of evidence that could prove Anqkar had not told the truth when he spoke with the police – he had not been with his partner, Linda Taylor, since the late 1980s.

A couple of days later, Matt called and confirmed that we had not received the full PNC data on Anqkar nor the complete police investigation logs. I looked back at the statements made by Zinzan, Dwyer and Makins and decided to look into Danny Dwyer, as his statement troubled me the most. I wanted to investigate how the Metropolitan Police handled cases concerning BAME officers and what involvement, if any, Dwyer had had with a controversial case against another Asian officer, DC Nabeel Akhtar.

What I found troubled me further. Headlines jumped out at me: 'Untouchables "nearly destroyed" undercover cop'. 'Asian detective's ordeal leads to calls for review'. 'Top Yard officers "fixed" case against colleague'.

It swiftly emerged that the Met's anti-corruption unit, the Complaints Investigation Bureau (CIB), had spent months of their time and hundreds of thousands of pounds secretly

tailing DC Akhtar but failed to find any evidence to bring a
case against him. Then, in January 2004, Akhtar had been
involved in a traffic incident after a minicab driver almost
crashed into his car at a junction. Five surveillance officers
from the anti-corruption squad, known as 'the Untouchables',
gave evidence claiming that they had seen Akhtar assaulting
the driver. Akhtar was convicted of common assault, but an
appeal court was subsequently shown CCTV footage that
showed the officers' testimony was gravely unreliable at best.
The judge said that he was 'wholly unable to accept' their
eyewitness evidence and demanded that Met Commissioner
Sir Ian Blair be passed a copy of his judgment. But nobody
at the Met notified the IPCC, and none of the officers was
suspended.

After reading all the articles, I contacted journalist and
author Michael Gillard, who had covered the Akhtar case.
He provided me with Akhtar's contact details. I tried to call
him, but there was no answer so I left a message. A few days
later, Akhtar called back and I explained my reasons for contacting him:

'I wanted to talk specifically about Danny Dwyer.'

'Be very careful,' Akhtar warned me. How can I help?'

'I want you to give evidence about what happened to you.'

'Sorry, mate, but I still have nightmares. I lost everything
– my wife, my business. Now I'm working abroad. That's why
it will have been difficult for you to get in contact with me.'

'Can you contact Matt, my solicitor? We just want to find
out what happened to you.'

'I can do better. I'll give him my solicitor's details so that he gets the full case file.'

'Brilliant!'

'Leave it with me. It's about time these people are dealt with. The DPS has a licence to destroy careers and they are backed up by the establishment. That's why I went abroad – after I left the Met they falsely accused me of a burglary. I have a new life now.'

A couple of evenings later, I received a message from Matt asking me to call him. He told me he had written to the prosecution requesting further disclosure, in particular on Makins, Dwyer and Zinzan, as discussed. I told Matt that it was my thirtieth wedding anniversary and I was taking Sathat to Barcelona for a few days to celebrate.

Before I left, I asked Matt to contact Theodore Fitzroy, a fellow ex-Met officer who had also been subjected to racial discrimination. Fitzroy's career ended following an employment tribunal in 1999.

Born in north London, but with parents from St Lucia, Fitzroy joined the Met in 1980 – two years before I did. After completing training school, Fitzroy was posted to Kentish Town and was one of only a handful of black officers to join the traffic division at the time. He followed this up with an eight-year stint on the child protection unit. I first met Fitzroy at BPA meetings in the early '90s, but our paths crossed again when his son and my daughter ended up in the same year at Oxford University. We became good friends and kept in touch, so when I called him he was willing to help.

On our return from Barcelona, Matt contacted me about his meeting with Fitzroy.

'How did it go?' I asked.

'OK. He [Fitzroy] walked me through the various forms and told me of the issues he had to deal with in the Met.'

'Did he tell you about his work with child protection?' Fitzroy was familiar with the Sapphire Unit and how they worked.

'Yes, he gave me a bit of background on how they operate, but, unfortunately, nothing relevant to our case.'

I asked about something else that had been bothering me while I was in Barcelona: 'On a different matter, Matt, we really need to show the jury the difference between a lock knife and a Stanley knife. Anqkar was convicted for carrying a lock knife, but in all of his accounts of the incident he claims that he carried a Stanley knife – there's a big difference between the two and we need the jury to understand that.'

'They'll know the difference.'

'I was telling my children and some councillors, and they'd never seen a lock knife.'

'Right, I see what you mean.'

'When people see a proper lock knife they'll know how dangerous it is. With Anqkar saying it was a Stanley knife, he's trying to lessen the impact of what he was convicted of.'

'I agree.'

'I'll get some pictures together and print them off,' I said. 'I'll also get pictures of the ASP.'

'OK, we can give them to the prosecution as well.'

'Are you aware Makins doesn't mention the knife at all?'

'Yes, he talks about arresting him for shoplifting.'

'Surely if Anqkar was arrested with a knife, then I would have taken it off him as the arresting officer?'

'Yes, Makins doesn't mention the knife.'

'We can discuss it with Henry.'

'One more thing: when Anqkar speaks to Doherty, he doesn't mention that the CRB check triggered his memory of the alleged assault. But that's what he told the police.'

'Good point.'

The following week, I went with Matt and Henry to a final pre-trial hearing at Southwark Crown Court, where we learnt that Judge Leonard would no longer be presiding over the case. We were given no reasons as to why this was and were told that we would find out who the new judge would be closer to the trial.

Afterwards, we went to a local coffee shop and sifted through the statements of Makins, Dwyer and Zinzan once again. Matt decided he didn't want to call my crime squad partner at the time of the alleged incident, Paul Mady, as a witness. Matt had still not secured a statement from Graham Markwick.

I told Matt to ask for my personnel file, as it would show that I hadn't been a police driver in 1986, as well as my annual appraisals. We also discovered that Makins had retired from Guernsey's police force before making his official witness statement, and therefore could not be subject to any misconduct proceedings.

There was still no Arrest Form 74 for October 1986. We confirmed that the arrest form and the fingerprints that the prosecution had sent Henry related to my arrest of Anqkar in 1987 for failing to appear at court for the October 1986 offence.

The month preceding the trial was hectic. Ten days before it was set to commence, I went to meet Matt at his office and we spent six hours going through all the statements one last time. The following Thursday, Sathat, Matt and I met Henry at his chambers to discuss the case. Henry informed us that the prosecution would no longer be calling Danny Dwyer as a witness, as a result, it seemed, of information relating to Akhtar's case. The van driver, Wildboar, had been traced and we would be receiving his full statement. The prosecution had also released Anqkar's psychiatric report and it was confirmed that David Zinzan would be giving evidence.

Other evidence we discussed included a new disclosure detailing DI Donna Smith's report to the IPCC, dated 23 June 2014:

> Mr Makins acknowledges that he did not report the attack at the time … He is now retired and works for local government in Guernsey. If he were still a serving officer, his actions of not reporting the assault may amount to gross misconduct despite the incident being over twenty years old … Mr Makins is currently a witness for the prosecution therefore any misconduct investigation would be subjudice.

'There was no statement from Geoffrey Mitchell,' Matt pointed out.

'That's because his evidence would have been in our favour. According to an email dated 3 July 2015 that Gadsby sent to himself, Gadsby had spoken to Anqkar and confirmed that Anqkar did make contact with Michael Doherty. Gadsby made contact with Doherty only to be redirected to his legal team, so he hung up,' I responded.

'The prosecution has accepted that Anqkar contacted Michael Doherty and confirms the conversation he had with him, so Doherty will not be called,' said Matt.

'That's a shame because he wanted to give evidence,' I said.

'Dr Richard Stone's statement has been accepted and he will not be required to attend court,' Matt said. 'DC Markwick's last-minute statement has also been received and accepted; he will not be required to attend court and his statement will be redacted.'

'Which bits are they redacting?' I asked.

'The prosecution wants any references to Tom Makins taken out,' said Henry.

'I haven't seen the statement. What does it say?' I asked.

'Graham states he does not have strong memories of Tom Makins, which of course supports your assertion that you cannot recall him either,' said Matt.

'I'm sure Paul Mady was my partner at the time,' I said. 'That's why he was at court with me when Anqkar was convicted. The Arrest Form 74 clearly states I arrested him for failing to appear, not for the original arrest in October. What does Graham say about the arrest?'

Matt then quoted what Graham had said in relation to his

name being shown on the conviction certificate as the arresting officer for Anqkar in 1986:

> I am recorded as the informant or complainant with a crime number 5347/86. That would be a 1986 crime reference number. I don't have any specific recollection of this case, although it seems clear that I must have been connected in some way. I am not certain what the specific role was, whether I was the interviewing officer, the arresting officer, or the officer in the case, but it seems from this record that I must have had that sort of connection to be listed in that way.

'If Graham cannot recall this, how am I supposed to remember it?' I argued.

Henry was worried about Makins and Zinzan; he needed time to think about how he would deal with both men. Matt was hesitant to call Fitzroy as a witness, as Fitzroy had taken the Met to a tribunal over racism and Matt knew that the prosecution would play on this.

I told Matt that it would be hard to find a BAME (Black, Asian and Minority Ethnic) officer who hadn't experienced racial discrimination while serving in the Met. Following tribunals, officers are asked to sign confidentiality agreements, which is why it's so difficult for BAME officers to talk about their cases in public. Although there had been a lot of pressure on us to sign such an agreement after my first case, Sathat and I had been adamant in our refusal to do so.

'Is that why they keep picking on you to discredit you?' asked Matt.

'Of course it is,' said Sathat. 'They asked me to sign as well but I refused, despite the Met offering me money. Gurpal believes that the truth needs to be told.'

'It is a good motive,' said Matt.

'By going for election, it will give Gurpal a platform to speak out against the injustices. Think about it: councillor, GLA member, MP – of course they are fearing this,' said Sathat.

'They will argue that Anqkar came to them and it was their duty to investigate,' said Henry.

'Then why aren't white officers who have beaten people up in the past being investigated?' I asked.

'The jury won't accept a conspiracy theory,' Henry pointed out.

On Friday 24 July, three days before the trial was due to start, we finally received full disclosure.

CHAPTER 14

INSIDE THE
GLASS CAGE

The day of the trial arrived.

On Monday 27 July 2015, my family and I headed to Southwark Crown Court. As soon as we arrived, I went to the canteen to meet Matt and Henry. This was the first and only chance we would have to review the new disclosure that had been issued to us late on Friday afternoon – we had just thirty minutes.

The first document that we reviewed was a statement from DI Donna Smith. It said that she had made contact with David Wildboar, the man Makins claimed had been driving the van when the alleged incident occurred. She detailed that Wildboar had left Battersea and moved to Croydon in 1984, concluding that Wildboar had not been behind the wheel as Makins had asserted. DI Smith discovered this information on 6 November 2013.

'OK, well, it's interesting that the van driver, David Wildboar, hadn't even been working at Battersea in 1986,' Matt said.

'Well, are you really surprised? It's just something else they've got wrong. Was there anything else of interest?' I responded.

'Well, the prosecution have just handed over the Gold Group minutes; Anqkar's medical report; Anqkar's statement in which he admits that he spoke to Michael Doherty, a statement from the social worker, Ms Fletcher; and a statement from DC Kevin Newton and DI Donna Smith,' Henry responded as he went through the papers.

'Kevin Newton, who was present at Anqkar's initial police interview with DC Hastings, confirms that Anqkar did not tell him that he started counselling,' said Matt.

'So Anqkar only told Doherty about the counselling, and not the police?' I asked.

'Looks like it. No notes from Sapphire to say they picked this up or cvcn pursued this line of investigation,' Matt replied.

'OK. Moving on: Anqkar's medical report confirms that he went to a psychologist on 11 November 2013 and the reason for his appointment is given as possible legal proceedings against the police,' said Henry.

There was an announcement on the Tannoy: 'All parties in the case of Virdi to court fourteen. All parties in the case of Virdi to court fourteen.'

We made our way into the court, where I was led into the defendant's dock. The dock officer entered from a side door and asked me to confirm my name, before shutting the door and leaving me in my glass cage. Following my 1998 trial, I've suffered from claustrophobia – I hate being in small, confined places. I wondered if it would be best to tell the judge about my phobia, but I was worried he would think I was lying. I decided it was best to keep quiet.

I looked over to my left and spotted Sathat, Kesar, Tasvir and other friendly faces seated in the public gallery. The judge who was presiding over my case was His Honour Judge Andrew Goymer. He addressed the two barristers: Henry Blaxland for the defence and Julian Evans for the prosecution, and asked if they were ready to proceed.

Henry was first to answer:

HB: 'We are, yes. There are a few matters that I would like to raise. Firstly, regarding the police witnesses whom the prosecution will no longer rely upon, the bad character application and the conversation the complainant had with another man. This has been served on the prosecution and I will hand you up a transcript.'

JE: 'May I pass up a document listing all the witnesses together with a copy of the jury bundle. I propose to read out all the names on the witness list, including Mr Zinzan's, although it may be that he is not called. Your Honour has a copy of the draft opening note.'

HHJ: 'Let's deal with the question of bail. Mr Virdi, please stand up. If you fail to attend, that is an offence under the bail act; the trial will also proceed without you. You must write down or supply to your counsel your name and address. Should you fall ill or have an accident – and I hope that neither of those two things occurs – then we will at least know where to start looking. I am sure you understand what I have said.'

GV: 'Yes, Your Honour, I understand. I'm sorry but I'm struggling to hear you.'

HHJ: 'Very well, I will speak a bit louder. Mr Evans, how long do you think the trial will take?'

JE: 'It may conclude within a week. – but I think it would be prudent to alert the jury of the chance that it could creep into next week.'

HHJ: 'I will rise briefly so that we can get the jury panel together.'

Judge Goymer addressed the jury: 'Ladies and gentlemen, before we start we will ballot the jury who try the case. This is a case concerning a former police officer; is there anybody among you who is a serving or former officer, or who has a family member who fits that description?'

One lady stated that her brother-in-law was a retired police officer – she was excused. Evans proceeded to read out the names of the witnesses – my name was also read out.

The clerk then said: 'Will the defendant please stand?'

I didn't catch what he was saying so Matt motioned with his hand for me to stand.

'Your Honour, I am having difficulty hearing you from here,' I said.

The judge asked the dock officer to open the door to the dock, so that I would be able to hear the proceedings. I thanked the judge inwardly, not only could I now hear clearly, but the space had also eased my claustrophobia.

The dock officer opened the door with his key. I then moved towards the door.

The judge addressed me: 'Gurpal Virdi, the names you are

about to hear are the jurors who may try you. If you wish to object to any of them, you must do so as they come to the book to be sworn in. Before they are sworn in your objection shall be heard.' He turned to the group of people, 'You are about to be sworn in. Please take the oath or the affirmation card in your hand.'

There were eight men and four women: nine were white Europeans and three were from ethnic minority backgrounds. Once sworn in, they must always sit in the same seat throughout the trial. The men and women who were not selected as part of the jury were asked to leave the court, and the clerk turned to address me.

The clerk addressed me, asking me to stand, before reading out what I had been charged with:

'Count one: indecent assault on a male person, contrary to section fifteen (1) of the Sexual Offences Act 1956. Gurpal Virdi, on a day unknown between the fourth of September 1986 and the thirty-first of December 1986, indecently assaulted Wasim Anqkar. How do you plead?'

'Not guilty, Your Honour,' I responded clearly.

'Count two: misconduct in a public office, contrary to common law. Gurpal Virdi, on a day unknown between the fourth of September 1986 and the thirty-first of December 1986 – while acting as a public officer, namely, a police constable – wilfully misconducted himself to such a degree as to amount to an abuse of the public's trust in him as the holder of his office in that, without reasonable excuse or justification, he assaulted and racially abused Wasim Anqkar at a time when the said Wasim Anqkar was his prisoner. How do you plead?'

'Not guilty, Your Honour,' I responded with determination.

'The defendant has pleaded not guilty to each of these counts; it is your charge to say, having heard all the evidence, whether the defendant is guilty or not guilty.'

The judge asked me to sit down, before turning his attention to the jury:

Members of the jury … I think it is always helpful for you to have some introductory remarks from the judge before the case starts. The traditional layout of the courtroom is that the jury box is at the side. Sometimes you may feel as if you are just spectators and this feeling is all the stronger if counsel and I forget ourselves and lapse into legal jargon. You are not spectators at all … The nature of trial by jury: it is important to understand what you are called upon to do. What you are taking part in is a trial, not an inquiry, an inquest or an investigation. Your charge is to listen to the evidence, to do so with an open and impartial mind and then, and only when you have heard all of it, to decide what it does and does not prove. Please resist the temptation to turn yourselves into amateur or armchair detectives. That is not why you are here. Your verdict must be based only on what you hear in the courtroom – remember the words 'according to the evidence'… You must not make your own enquiries, as no one is able to check their accuracy.

You must not research this case on the internet. The internet has many useful functions; however, there are websites that do not provide accurate information. We cannot conduct a fair trial if jurors are influenced by anything other than the evidence they hear in the courtroom. You must not talk about the case with anyone other than your fellow jurors for the duration of the trial. You must not allow anybody to talk to you about it. You must not speak about the case outside of the court, as you never know who you might be speaking with or who might be listening. We have as many as fourteen courts trying cases in this building. Please do not talk to any of the other jurors.

The real danger comes when you go home, anybody who lives with you or who sees you in the evening will ask you questions about the case and, inevitably, they will want to give you their opinion – this is human nature. However, this is not helpful, in fact, it is positively dangerous. They have heard none of the evidence first hand and you may only have heard part of it. Just tell them you are not allowed to talk about it.

Don't even talk about this case amongst yourselves when you might be overheard. It's not even a good idea to talk about this case when all of you are not together. There are twelve of you; all twelve of you will have to make a decision.

There are certain things you must not do. They are punishable with imprisonment or a fine:

- To communicate with anybody about the case;
- To obtain any information about this case that is not part of the evidence in court;
- To reveal anything that went on in the jury room. You must keep this secret for ever.

If anything does happen during the course of the trial that upsets you, I need to know about it as soon as possible. There are two specific situations which you must look out for:

- If anybody tries to talk to you about the case;
- If anybody gets hold of information from a source outside of the court.

If either happens, tell me. Don't delay, as, like many things in life, it will only get worse if you do. If you leave it until after the verdict, it will be too late. I hope it is now clear why I have asked you not to take documents away with you.

At the beginning of your jury service you are shown a DVD. I have seen it myself, although not recently, but that doesn't matter. The format of a criminal trial is this: the prosecution starts by making an opening speech, which addresses:

- What the case is all about;
- What the prosecution must prove;
- How they say they will prove it with evidence.

Witnesses are questioned or examined by the prosecution; they are cross examined by the defence. The defendant may the give evidence, and he may call witnesses on his behalf, although he need do neither of those things. I will then sum up and you will go away to consider your verdict.

That's quite enough by way of introduction. Mr Evans?

CHAPTER 15

THE TEN LIES
OF ANQKAR

Wasim Kumi Uongo Anqkar walked into court. He looked as if he weighed a huge amount, particularly given he was of slightly below average height. He was dressed casually, as if he had just come from work, and had short, cropped hair. This was the first time I was seeing my accuser in real life. I didn't recognise him at all.

Evans began by asking Anqkar to recall the alleged incident, before leading him through his evidence. As Anqkar began talking, I started to make notes.

'My date of birth is 29 August 1970. I am forty-four years old.' Anqkar spoke with a south London accent, which reminded me of the way boxer Frank Bruno talked when being interviewed by TV commentator Harry Carpenter.

In my youth, I lived in London in the Battersea area. I was convicted of possession of an offensive weapon in a public place. In March 2013, I was interviewed by police in relation to events that occurred on that particular occasion. I provided an account in March 2013 about events of that day, and have made a number of witness statements, as part of a police investigation into those matters.

The first statement was made in July 2014; I have made others more recently, including during this year. In the course of the process, I was shown some documents to assist with dates.

In relation to my conviction certificate, dated 23 July 1987, I do recognise the address: that was the address where I lived with my brother. I am not known as 'Henry Anqkar'. The weapon was a Stanley knife. The offence was committed on 31 October 1986. On that day, I was sixteen years old … I was coming back from work experience in Clapham. I had been plastering and dry-lining. By that stage, I was about a week into it. It lasted two weeks. I jumped on the bus back to St John's Hill. It was about 6 or 7 p.m., it was October and it was dark.

I saw a guy named Michael, a friend of mine, and we had a chat. A neighbour of mine called Denzel walked past us and told me to fuck off. Denzel was known to me and he was a bully. I told him I wasn't going nowhere. He said he was going to beat me up and started walking towards me; he had his fists clenched. I took a few steps back, produced my Stanley knife and told him not to touch me. The Stanley knife was part of my work kit; it was an old-fashioned type with a blade that can be retracted. I showed it to him and he backed off; I then ran down the hill, down Plough Lane. Denzel did not follow me. I then heard shouting from across the road. Two guys wearing normal clothes ran over and shouted: 'Stop, Police!' I got grabbed and told to stand still. I had seen them earlier standing outside the Granada Bingo Hall. I found out their names: one was George Virdi, the other one was called Tom. I learnt their names at that stage, because they were talking to each other.

George grabbed me. He held me by my arm. Tom went off to speak to Denzel. When George grabbed me, he said: 'Where is the knife?' I said: 'It's in my pocket, here it is.' I gave it to him. I was put in the back of the van. Tom then came back to where I was with George. Tom said he wasn't pressing charges: I understood him to be referring to Denzel. We were probably thirty or forty metres from where the incident started. I hadn't heard anyone calling for a police van. It was a white Sherpa van; it was marked, the back doors were double doors. I'm sure it was Tom who got in first, I got in second and George got in behind. I had seen the driver of the van.

It was a transit van with two benches along the sides. It had a high top. You could stand up in it. There was a partition by the driver. There was no holding area or cage. When I got inside, George handcuffed me. The doors were shut. The handcuffs were old-fashioned ones, with a chain between the cuffs. There was one light inside the van. It was right in the middle. You could see bodies, but you couldn't see the colour of people's eyes. George asked me what my name was. I said that it was Harry Anqkar. He smacked me across my face with his hand. It was a down slap, downward strike, very hard. I was seeing stars. He said: 'What kind of name is that for a fucking nigger?' It just escalated from there. He started beating, punching [and] kicking [me] – he was trying to get me in a head-lock. My hands were in front of me, handcuffed.

He was trying to grab me around the head. He wasn't able to put me into the sleeper position, where he'd have my windpipe. This was because I'd had self-defence train-ing. The way to stop somebody doing that is by pulling your neck down into your shoulder. I had self-defence training probably a month before, at the local gym or lei-sure centre. When he realised he couldn't get my windpipe and couldn't strangle me, he started beating me on the back of my head and on the back of my neck, kneeing me in my chest. It was designed to hurt me. He punched me fifteen or twenty times. [His punches were] directed to my stomach, my back; I was bent over. There were none to my face. It seemed like it lasted for fifteen minutes but, in fact, it was probably five minutes. It took from Plough Road to the bottom of Clapham Junction. When we turned left into Falcon Road, that's when I kicked the door open.

Tom, the other officer, was also inside the van. Tom had jumped on top of the bench in the right-hand corner. He had to get out of the way because of the way George flung me round with the handcuffs. I was touching every panel of the van except the roof.

Tom started screaming out for him to leave me alone, for him to get off. He said: 'Get off him, George! Why are you fucking doing this? You're fucking killing him! Why are you doing this?' He was screaming and shouting at the top of his voice. Those words had no effect at all on George. Tom didn't try to intervene physically. I got tired and lost my footing. I was on my back with my hands up in the air, above my head. He [George] was actually sitting in the rowing position, pulling on the handcuffs. He put his feet on my shoulders. He was pulling the handcuffs. I was screaming out in pain. I rolled on to my left side; I was in the foetal position. I was sliding to the doors. I was picked up by my waist; I felt pressure on my side. I felt a sharp pain in my backside. I realised he was shoving something up my anus. I thought it was his thumb that he was doing it with. It continued for about ten seconds. I was in a lot of pain. I kicked my right leg out. I had a pair of shell bottoms on; it was a tracksuit made out of nylon. I was wearing underwear. I got sheer pain in my anus. When he stopped, I saw something in his hand. When he inserted it up my anus, I was kicking the van doors – I managed to kick them wide open.

I was stunned by what I heard coming out of Anqkar's mouth; his recollection of what had happened seemed so far from the truth. Anqkar went on:

That's when Tom banged on the partition for the driver to stop. The van stopped right at the bridge in Clapham Junction at Falcon Road. When I kicked the doors open, the van was in motion. It stopped. All I could see was day-light coming into the van. I could see ten, fifteen people standing at the bus stop staring at me, wondering what was going on. I turned around. George was like a rabbit in the headlights. He wasn't expecting the doors to open up.

The object was a small collapsible truncheon. It was black and made of metal. It was like the top of a golf club handle, but not as long. It was ten inches long. It was in its collapsible form. I had seen one on television before this incident; it was a standard issue for the German police. I'd seen them use one in a football match. The attack stopped once the doors were open. The driver ran around to slam the doors closed. The van moved on. We ended up going to Battersea police station.

They picked me up off the floor and put me on the bench. They were talking about the door being kicked open: that had never happened before. I said to them that I couldn't believe they'd done this to a fifteen-year-old. I was sixteen at the time. George replied: 'What's your date of birth? What's your fucking date of birth?' I gave them my date of birth. I told them I'd let everybody know: I'd say it in interview and also to my dad, what they had done to me. I could tell they were very worried when they realised I was a minor. I formed that view because of the way they were looking at each other. My impression was that they were thinking: 'How are we going to get out of this?'

They escorted me out of the van, up the stairs and into the police station. I was processed by a custody sergeant.

I gave my name and address and they took all my possessions out of my pockets. I was sent to the cells after I'd given my details. This was the custody sergeant telling me to go to the cell. I told him that that wasn't the procedure, that somebody was supposed to take me there. I made my way to the cell; I was very frightened. I looked around the corner. As I looked around, George and Tom were standing by the cell door, growling, showing their teeth, clenching their fists – like gargoyles. I started a bit of small talk with them, saying they'd done enough already. I got one step away from George; I launched myself towards him, took one step towards him, one to the side and ran in. Before I got in, George grabbed my jacket. I just let it go. He was trying to drag me out with it. The door remained open for about twenty seconds. I displayed to them that if they came in, then I would go down fighting. What happened in the van wasn't going to happen again. I remained in the cell until later on that evening.

I was taken out to be fingerprinted and photographed. I was waiting for my dad; he's my stepfather rather than my biological father. He came to the police station.

They came to the cell – well, I think George opened the cell door and Tom was standing behind him – and they told me I was being released. They took me to the foyer and told me I was free to go. They told my father to keep me out of trouble – well, more George than Tom. I wasn't interviewed at all.

I met my dad. I went down the stairs and I told my

stepfather that they'd beaten me up really badly and that [George] had stuck his truncheon up my arse. That conversation took place outside the building. My dad reacted as if he didn't believe me. He just looked at me and carried on walking like I didn't say anything. There was no concern. If my son said something like that to me, I know what I'd do: I'd go back into that police station. Because I wasn't his real son, he didn't do anything about it.

It was obvious that Anqkar was playing to the jury, trying to pull on their heartstrings and garner some sympathy.

I wasn't charged. I went to court about the possession of an offensive weapon. I first went some months later, probably around six months later. I went to Lambeth East Juvenile Court or rather Balham Juvenile Court as I knew it to be. I pleaded not guilty. There was a trial. I had a solicitor representing me at the trial. George was a witness against me. He gave evidence. Tom had left the force by then. I was found guilty.

Prior to these matters in April, I was arrested a second time by George. He arrested me, basically, for standing outside a car. It was parked at the bottom of Cologne Road. We were all standing around this car. He pulled up in his Mini Metro, asked me whose car it was and I told him it was mine. He said: 'You're nicked, you're not old enough to drive the car, get in the car.' I asked George why I was being arrested. I asked why he kept harassing me. The last question I asked was where the nice officer who helped me out in the van was – I meant Tom. George replied that he 'fucking couldn't hack it, he resigned.' I can't remember exactly when this was.

On another occasion, I did see George with a truncheon. It was before April, before I was convicted. He used to drive by in his car, tapping on the window, pulling funny faces, trying to wind us up – acting like a goat. When he tapped [the truncheon] on the window, I knew what he was saying – only me and him knew what that truncheon meant.

He spoke to me on a few occasions. After what he done to me, he never acted violently, but every time he pulled me over – three or four times a week – if I had friends with me, he'd search all my friends, but he wouldn't search me. He'd put me on the side, [but] he'd search the others from top to bottom. When he found nothing on them, he said to them they were free to go. I thought it was strange, and my friends said: 'Why hasn't he searched you?' He wasn't searching me because he wanted it to appear as if I was a police informer. He was messing with my head. He knew what it would look like.

As for my injuries, my wrists were in bad, bad shape – terrible shape. They'd swollen to about three times their size. It was almost like I had make-up, lady's eyeliner, on my wrist. It was metal – he'd burnt marks into my skin. I had pain in my anus. My ribs were bruised; it was hard for me to walk. I hadn't seen any medical practitioner in the station.

I never saw Tom again. George stopped me regularly for about four or five months – up until the trial. I saw him on a few occasions after the trial. Before the court case, I saw him again when I was on my own. He pulled up and told me to jump in. He offered me a brown envelope every month to be a police informer. He offered me that just once. I told him I didn't want that; I was a working man. He told me I would do what he wanted me to do. This was in 1987.

After the court case, I saw him when he came to the youth club, where there was a big disco. We were all waiting outside, smoking cigarettes and drinking beer, waiting for everyone to disperse. Someone said: 'Look, it's George's car.' I automatically ducked down on my hands and knees, hiding. I didn't actually see him – all I saw was his car. That was in 1987. That was the last time I saw him for years.

I next saw him in Tooting, in 2007. I was driving down Tooting Bec High Road and saw somebody acting a bit strange, looking at a display outside a stall. I thought I knew him from somewhere. I was going to work. He turned around, looked straight at me and I thought: 'Ah still working, mate.' He couldn't recognise me. I'm much heavier now; I was eleven stone then.

I was thinking to myself that if I came up with what happened to me, nobody would believe me – two officers against one civilian. I know Tom was trying to help me, but I thought he'd stick by George. The reason I didn't report anything in 1986 was because nobody would believe me. It was outrageous, it was shocking. I spoke to a social worker friend about what happened and as a result went to speak to the police. I reported matters to the police a few months before March 2013 to explain what happened – I was told to come back.

I am presently in a relationship with Linda Taylor. I started my relationship with her in late 1987 or 1988. When I first met her, I told her straight away that I couldn't go to Battersea because I was being harassed by an Asian officer. I told her I had been beaten up in the back of a van. I didn't tell her that he sodomised me. I did have that conversation with her about five years later. It was in the early 1990s.

I stepped out of the glass cage and went to join my family. No one said much on the way home, as we were all shocked by Anqkar's outrageous allegations. At home I made tea and we went through our notes.

'He was clearly not telling the truth,' said Kesar.

'Why take the Stanley knife out of his toolbox at work?' I said.

Kesar was quick to spot the inconsistencies in Anqkar's story: 'He said daylight came into the van, but at the same time he says this incident happened in the evening. He's clearly contradicting himself.'

'That's because he had made the whole thing up, Kesar,' I sighed.

Kesar couldn't believe Anqkar was coming out with such blatant lies: 'He also got confused and at different points in his account he said he was both fifteen and sixteen – how can you not know how old you are?'

'This is something for Henry to pick up on in the cross examination,' I responded.

That night I scoured the internet to see if I could find any information about ASPs being used in Germany, but I was unsuccessful. I then turned my attention to Anqkar's comments about his age. In Anqkar's initial police interview and statement, he had claimed that he'd been fifteen when the alleged assault occurred, yet he had changed his tune in court by saying that he was in fact sixteen at the time. I found this hard to believe and I was keen for Henry to hammer this point home in court.

● ● ●

The following day, I was back in my glass cage with the dock officer sitting behind me. I had my notepad ready with a pen in my right hand. Would Henry expose Anqkar?

Henry stood up, pulling his gown over his shoulders.

HB: 'You moved from one employer to another and there had to be a security check?'
WA: 'Yes.'
HB: 'An inquiry with the Criminal Records Bureau, a CRB check was done?'
WA: 'Yes.'

HB: 'You got this document and that document reminded you of the events back in the 1980s?'

WA: 'Yes.'

HB: 'That brought it all back to you, the CRB check?'

WA: 'Yes.'

HB: 'That was in 2011?'

WA: 'Yes.'

HB: 'Late 2012?'

Anqkar explained that media coverage of Jimmy Savile's sexual abuse had prompted him to make his allegations. He said he had been formally interviewed by the police on 13 March 2013, but that it had not been until 1 July 2014 that he'd made a formal statement. Anqkar said that before making this statement, he'd made a phone call to Michael Doherty. He said he knew Doherty had recorded the call and said he'd been told by the police that Doherty had spoken to my solicitor. Anqkar said he had made a further statement to the police in September 2014. Anqkar also revealed that he had spoken to a psychotherapist in November 2013.

HB: 'When you gave evidence yesterday you told His Honour and the jury that after you had been seriously assaulted by my client, Mr Virdi, in the back of the police van, first of all you said you told them you were fifteen years old?'

WA: 'Yes.'

HB: 'And went on to say that "when I get interviewed I am going to tell everyone what you have done to me?"'
WA: 'Yes.'
HB: 'In none of the accounts you gave to various people is that you said in the back of that van that "when I get interviewed I am going to tell everyone". The first time that you said that was in this court, do you agree with that?'
WA: 'In a way I agree.'
HB: 'Had you ever mentioned it before or not?'
WA: 'At some point I did mention that when the attack stopped and they put me on the bench, I said that I am fifteen and I am going to let my dad know when I am interviewed.'

Henry asked him if he had told the custody sergeant at Battersea police station what had happened. Anqkar said he hadn't told the sergeant because he knew he was going to be interviewed and he planned to describe what had happened when his father was present. He said he had told his father he'd been assaulted. But Henry pointed out that a female officer, who had spoken to Anqkar on 5 March, had written a note saying 'he didn't tell anyone about the assault at the time the assault took place.'

HB: 'Did you tell your father that you didn't like Indians?'
WA: 'Yes.'
HB: 'When was that?'
WA: 'About 2007, I think.'

HB: 'The time you told him about what happened?'

WA: 'The time I reminded him about what happened.'

HB: 'Did you tell your father about this for the first time after you made the formal complaint to police and came forward?'

WA: 'No.'

HB: 'You say you told him way before that?'

WA: 'Yes.'

HB: 'And you told him you did not like Indians at the same time?'

WA: 'I told him that I did not like Indians because of what this man has done to me.'

Henry dismissed Anqkar's assertion that he had told his solicitor about the alleged assault, calling the claim a 'pack of lies'. Then Henry asked Anqkar about what had happened after he'd left the police station. Anqkar admitted to having received a letter summoning him to appear in court. Henry pointed out that Anqkar had failed to turn up at court voluntarily, he had been arrested, held overnight and then taken to court. Henry suggested Anqkar held a grudge against me, as I was the officer who had arrested him for his no-show in court. Anqkar denied he had been arrested and claimed he had walked into court under his 'own steam'.

It was at this stage that the judge intervened to ask Anqkar to confirm he had voluntarily surrendered.

HHJ: You voluntarily surrendered?

WA: Yes.

HB: The arresting officer, PC Virdi, arrested you for failing to appear and looks like you were held overnight. Have you spent a night in custody?

WA: Yes.

HB: Have you spent a night in custody around this time, in 1987?

WA: No.

Anqkar tried not to make eye contact with Henry or the jury; instead he fixed his gaze on the paperwork in front of him. Henry changed his line of questioning, asking Anqkar if he had ever been married. Anqkar replied that he hadn't.

HB: 'What did you do on your twenty-first birthday?'

WA: 'I can't remember.'

HB: 'You got married, didn't you?'

WA: 'Married? No sir.'

HB: [Pointing to what appears to be a marriage certificate] 'That mean anything to you?'

Henry handed Anqkar the document, which Anqkar glanced at in horror. He shook his head, before grabbing his glass of water and taking a gulp. Jury members were staring at him intently now, and some looked angry. In a low voice, Anqkar admitted that he had got married on his twenty-first birthday to a lady called Leah Caraboo, whom he had met through his auntie.

HB: Why did you tell the court you had never been married?

WA: Because, to be honest, it went from my memory.

HB: It was a lie, wasn't it? That is the problem, isn't it, you are prepared to lie?

My family members were delighted at the sight of Anqkar being broken down by Henry, who then moved on to another subject.

HB: 'Linda Taylor, who you have been with for many years, is she the same Linda Taylor to whom you transferred your property in early 2000? You became bankrupt and as a result you appeared in court charged with transferring property?'

WA: 'Yes.'

HB: 'You have a conviction for transferring property to her in the five years before you were declared bankrupt – that is straightforwardly dishonest?'

WA: 'We were in a high mortgage. To get a lower mortgage rate so I could afford a mortgage – that is why I did that.'

HB: 'You were pretending the property was not yours by transferring it into her name?'

WA: 'I needed to get a lower mortgage.'

At last, Anqkar was being exposed as a liar, something that should have already been done by the police.

Henry turned to the phone call Anqkar had made to Michael Doherty. Henry said that Anqkar had told Doherty he planned to sue the police. Anqkar denied this, but when the judge then intervened and asked Anqkar whether he had planned to sue the police, Anqkar admitted that he had. Next, Henry turned to Anqkar's sessions with his psycho-therapist, Mr Andrews.

> HB: 'You told him this, or he notes: "Mr Anqkar initially began talking about his reasons for wanting an assess-ment". This was a psychiatric assessment "which related to possible legal proceedings following a previous incident where he described himself as a victim of sexual assault by a police officer with the Metropolitan Police Service."'
> WA: 'Yes.'
> HB: 'This is why you went to him, to provide you with a report to help you in possible legal proceedings – you are just a gold digger?'
> WA: 'No, it was because of my state of mind.'

Henry then outlined the inconsistencies in Anqkar's ac-counts of the alleged assault against him, pointing out that at first he had made no mention of having burn marks on his wrists. Initially, he had only told officers at the station that his wrists were swollen.

> HB: 'You told Mr Doherty that Mr Virdi had assaulted you on what you describe as your pressure points with his truncheon: "He had a collapsible truncheon, on my pressure points, it makes you jump like a dog when it hits

you." You told Mr Doherty that he used his truncheon to hit your pressure points?'

WA: 'I told him that I think he used something to hit my pressure points. When he was laying his hands on me the pain was too much.'

HB: 'There was nothing about that in your evidence to the police or in court?'

WA: 'No.'

HB: 'Do you want to change your evidence?'

WA: 'I can't say he did, as I did not see him using it.'

HB: 'Why tell Mr Doherty?'

WA: 'The only way I could tell how he was giving me so much pain, he had to be using something. It could not just be his hands or his fingers.'

HB: 'He was prodding you?'

WA: 'Yes, it felt like he was prodding me.'

HB: 'Where are your pressure points?'

WA: 'In your neck, in here.'

HB: 'You know this from your self-defence training?'

WA: 'Yes.'

HB: 'Have you just made this up?'

WA: 'I felt like he was using something but I never saw it.'

Henry asked Anqkar about Samantha Fletcher, whom Anqkar had described as a social worker in his initial police interview. Following media reports of the sexual abuse committed by TV star Jimmy Savile, Anqkar had been prompted to go and see Ms Fletcher.

HB: 'And you told her about someone you describe as an Asian officer, and you said to her that she would know who you were talking about, because he had got a lot of money from the police as he had not been promoted because he was Asian? That is what you told her?'

WA: 'Yes.'

HB: 'What did you know about him?'

WA: 'What I had seen in the newspaper.'

HB: 'What?'

WA: 'That he had been awarded compensation.'

HB: 'How much?'

WA: '£200,000.'

HB: 'You told Mr Doherty that you thought it was £300,000.'

WA: 'OK.'

HB: 'When spoken to by Mr Newton in that video interview, did you tell him about what you knew about Gurpal Virdi's case?'

WA: 'No.'

HB: 'You told him you had seen him in Tooting?'

WA: 'Yes.'

HB: 'You didn't say that you had seen him in the news and that he had received a lot of money?'

WA: 'No.'

HB: 'Why didn't you mention that?'

WA: 'It had no relevance. What he got is between him and the police.'

HB: 'It was relevant to you to mention that to PC Newton.

You mentioned that your friend had seen him on the
television.'

WA: 'Yes, it was another person.'

HB: 'You thought that was relevant. Why not say that you
had seen him in the press and that you knew he had got a
lot of money out of the police?'

WA: 'I was not asked, and I did not think it was relevant.'

HB: 'It would have given the game away, good old-
fashioned gold digging?'

WA: 'No.'

Henry then turned his attention to the Metropolitan Police
Commissioner at the time, Sir Bernard Hogan-Howe, and
Anqkar's assertions of his involvement in the case.

HB: 'Conversations you have had with the police since you
first spoke to them, were you ever told by a police officer
that as part of their investigation that the Metropolitan
Police Commissioner had become involved, Bernard
Hogan-Howe, and had personally travelled to Australia or
Canada to personally interview Tom Makins?'

WA: 'I did say that.'

HB: 'Why?'

WA: 'I said that a high-up police officer, I thought it might
be Sir Bernard Hogan-Howe.'

HB: 'You had been told that by somebody?'

WA: 'Yes.'

HB: 'Who?'

WA: 'One of the officers. He did not say that it was Bernard Hogan-Howe, he said a senior police officer; he was taking a long-haul flight.'

HB: 'Who?'

WA: 'A police officer. I can't remember.'

HB: 'PC Newton was your main point of call?'

WA: 'Could have been him.'

HB: 'Did you say that to Mr Doherty to [try to] impress him in order to get him to take your case?'

WA: 'No.'

HHJ: 'You did say to him that a senior police officer, possibly the commissioner himself?'

WA: 'Yes.'

HHJ: 'And did you mention Australia?'

WA: 'Yes, I might have done. It was a long-haul flight.'

HB: 'Read the transcript of what you said.'

[WA reads]

WA: 'Yes.'

As I listened to Anqkar's responses to Henry, the inconsistencies and lies in his evidence seemed to only increase. Henry then returned to October 1986, the time of the alleged incident.

HB: 'October 1986. What you told the police consistently in your interviews and your statement was that at that time you were living at home with your parents at Brussels Road?'

WA: 'I said between places.'

HB: 'You did not say that. What you said at the time was that you were living at home with your parents in Brussels Road?'

WA: 'Yes.'

HB: 'And that is not far from Plough Road?'

WA: 'No.'

HB: 'Tab three, p. 6, Form 74C. An antecedents form in your name. The OIC is said to be Gurpal Virdi with the name George crossed out. Date is 9 July 1987 and it records under paragraph ten [officer's notes] "that at the time of your arrest you were residing at Brussels Road. He has always given the address of Effra Road when stopped and spoken to, and it is believed this is his correct address".'

WA: 'Yes.'

Henry asked Anqkar if he could recall any occasion when I had harassed him or tried to get him to become a police informant. Anqkar claimed that this was why he had moved home from Brussels Road to Effra Road. Henry challenged this; if Anqkar had been living in Effra Road as per the Arrest Form 74, then his claim that he moved due to the harassment couldn't be true.

HB: 'That was the explanation you were giving [to Michael Doherty] – moving to get out of the way of the wicked Gurpal Virdi?'

WA: 'Yes.'

HB: 'It was a complete lie. You were already living in Effra Road?'
WA: 'No.'

After further questioning, concerning Anqkar's general testimony, Henry moved on to the issue of Anqkar's age. Henry argued that Anqkar had wanted police to believe he was fifteen; he had intentionally lied in order to appear underage at the time of the alleged incident. But what Anqkar hadn't realised was that definitive records regarding his age existed – Anqkar denied this charge.

When asked whether he struggled, Anqkar claimed that he didn't attempt to fight back as he was handcuffed and he knew that it would only serve to aggravate the situation, but he did try to dodge any blows that were directed at him.

Henry pointed out that Anqkar had initially claimed he'd been resisting and struggling, and had tried to move around the back of the van to stop himself being cornered and hit. Holding up an ASP – the collapsible truncheon Anqkar claimed I'd used to assault him – to the court, Henry explained that ASPs had not been issued by the Met until the 1990s.

The fact that I had not been an authorised police driver and therefore could not have picked Anqkar up in a police vehicle car and drive him around, as he alleged, was pointed out to Anqkar by Henry. 'Do you want to change your answer?' he asked Anqkar.

'When I was arrested, he was in the back with me,' Anqkar insisted.

Anqkar was by now broken down and exposed as a complete liar in front of the court. Henry called Anqkar's claims a 'pack of lies'.

Anqkar's barrister, Mr Julian Evans, then began his re-examination. Anqkar told Mr Evans he had not mentioned his allegations to the custody sergeant at the time, because my partner and I were there, and he also didn't think the sergeant would believe him – Anqkar claimed he had been 'under duress'. He denied that his claims were just a 'pack of lies'. He also denied having a grudge against me, and said that his allegations against me had not been triggered by a desire to make money.

The judge then asked about the conversations that Anqkar had had with Michael Doherty, including the fact that Anqkar had approached several solicitors but no solicitor would take his case up. Anqkar confirmed this to the judge. Anqkar denied that he had told Doherty he wanted to sue the police.

Thomas Makins was the next witness. He was an inch short of six feet, and of medium build, with an average-length haircut. He was wearing a suit and, judging by his healthy glow, he'd recently been on holiday – while I had been facing one of the biggest battles of my life. The last time I'd seen Makins had been in 1987 and now, looking at him, I felt nothing but anger towards him. But I was in court, so I had to stay calm.

Makins, who had resigned from the Met in May 1987, told the court he was now working as a mental health case manager in Guernsey, following his retirement from the police force in 2013 (he had been an inspector). Originally joining the Met as a cadet in 1979, Makins became a constable in 1981 and was posted to Battersea. According to Makins, he and I had worked together on the Battersea crime squad from roughly January 1986 to February/March 1987 – the crime squad were generally concerned with street robberies such as pickpocketing and handbag snatching. Makins also said that when investigating officers gave him disclosure, he knew, almost as a premonition, that it was about Kumi Uongo 'Harry' Anqkar, whom he described as a police 'nominal' – someone who is believed to be a petty criminal operating in the area.

Makins said that after arresting Anqkar, we had planned to take him to Battersea police station. It was apparently PC Wilder or Wildboar who had driven the van that arrived to collect Anqkar. Makins went on to claim that a minute, or two minutes, into the journey, Anqkar started making 'some sort of comment' about us arresting him, which set me off and I went over to where Anqkar was sitting and a tussle or fight started.

'Mr Virdi grabbed him, grappled with him. I would say it was a 25-year-old man overpowering a fourteen-year-old boy,' Makins told the court. 'I don't recall any big punching or big kicking going on, it was just pure force to grapple, wrestle with Mr Anqkar.'

Makins claimed he had intervened to separate us because he'd thought I 'was using excessive force to detain a fourteen- or fifteen-year-old youth who was handcuffed in the back of a police van and was not posing any real threat'.

Makins said that after escorting Anqkar to a cell at Battersea police station, he'd not seen him again that evening. He told the court he had not seen any injuries to Anqkar, and he could not recall Anqkar complaining about injuries. He said old-fashioned wooden truncheons had been available to police at the time, but he'd never seen a collapsible truncheon. Henry showed Makins a modern ASP; it had been a brilliant decision to take one of these collapsible truncheons into the court. I could tell that seeing it made an impact on the jury.

'I never saw any member of the crime squad ever in possession of such an item,' Makins told the court. 'That would include Mr Virdi. I did not see a uniformed or plain-clothes officer with one. I did not see Mr Virdi with any unauthorised equipment. The first time I saw an ASP was when I transferred to Guernsey.'

The next day, Gehazi Sautelabaap, Anqkar's stepfather, was the first person to give evidence. His poor eyesight meant that he had trouble reading the oath. He was a small man and very scruffy and unkempt, considering that he worked as a case worker for the Home Office. He told the court he'd become Anqkar's stepfather in 1974. At times, while giving his evidence, Sautelabaap seemed confused. Henry asked him when Anqkar had given him my name. Sautelabaap replied that it had been after he went to the police.

'The police came to me in 2013 and I gave the statement. Since the police referred the issue I got them to ask a few questions and I spoke to him after that,' he told the court.

Then it was Linda Taylor's turn to enter the witness box. Dressed in a casual top and jeans, Linda was on the thin side. Her short hair was tied up in a ponytail. She said she'd begun a serious relationship with Anqkar in 1988 and that in

1989, or 1990, he had told her about a time when the police had arrested him. Basically, she told much the same story as Anqkar had told, and I wondered whether someone had been coaching her. Henry asked her if she was still living with Anqkar and she replied that she was. He asked her if Anqkar had ever said he was thinking of suing the police. She claimed that Anqkar had never said this.

> HB: 'In 2004, when living in Lancashire, Harry transferred a property to you?'
> CB: 'Yes.'
> HB: 'Why?'
> CB: 'Just to get a mortgage.'
> HB: 'He was in money troubles at the time?'
> CB: 'Yes.'
> HB: 'In debt?'
> CB: 'We all are.'
> HB: 'He was declared bankrupt?'
> CB: 'Yes.'
> HB: 'And he was prosecuted for transferring the property to you – he has a criminal conviction?'
> CB: 'Yes.'
> HB: 'Was that a dishonest attempt to get money?'
> CB: 'No, it was for a deposit.'
> HB: 'Did you know he was married?'

We had all been waiting for this question. Even the jury members stopped writing to look at her. But Taylor had clearly been waiting for the question too. She remained calm and unflustered.

CB: 'Yes.'
HB: 'He told you about it?'
CB: 'Yes, we were on a break years ago.'

According to Anqkar, when giving evidence, he'd had no memory of his marriage until Henry produced the marriage certificate. Yet, Taylor knew that he was married. This implied that they had been discussing the case overnight, and everybody in the courtroom knew it.

Henry sat down. It had been a great finale to his cross examination. Taylor left the dock looking as if she had been short-changed; she'd been eager to confirm Anqkar's story, but had not been given the opportunity to do so. Henry had finished her off.

The next witness to be called was Detective Sergeant David Gadsby, who stood up confidently to take the oath. But I could tell that he knew he was going to be in for a hard time. Previously Gadsby had held the upper hand, but now he would have to justify his methods, his investigation and his conduct.

HB: 'How long have you been a police officer?'
DG: 'Twenty-one years.'
HB: 'We can see from the conviction record that the conviction recorded against Harry Anqkar was for a lock knife?'
DG: 'Yes.'

This was important as Anqkar had claimed several times that he had been arrested for carrying a Stanley knife.

> HB: 'Have you had experience of arresting people in possession of a lock knife?'
>
> DG: 'I can't specifically recall, but I am sure I have done.'
>
> HB: 'I want to make a point that there can be no confusion between a lock knife and a Stanley knife. Can you look at these two graphics – these accurately show the difference between the two?'
>
> DG: 'They do, but it is also right that a Stanley knife does lock into place.'

There were audible gasps from the jury and from some people sitting in the public gallery, as there was no mistaking the significant difference in size between the two knives. A Stanley knife was an everyday DIY tool, while a lock knife was often carried by street gangs. How could Gadsby fail to have spotted this significant inconsistency between official court records and Anqkar's claims? The judge glanced at David Gadsby, whose confidence seemed to have vanished into thin air. Gadsby suddenly appeared to be nervous.

> HB: 'If you were to arrest someone for a Stanley knife, you would record it as a Stanley knife?'
>
> DG: 'I cannot say what the person writing this would have thought.'

HB: 'What would you say when arresting someone for this?'

DG: 'Stanley knife.'

Henry continued to ask probing questions. Gadsby was starting to look clearly embarrassed; his face had turned red. He did not seem to want to look at the jury and instead kept glancing at his lawyer, Julian Evans, probably in some vain hope that Evans might intervene. But Gadsby was all on his own now and would have to justify his poor investigation. There were no senior police officers here to intervene on his behalf. Henry asked Gadsby whether Anqkar's claim that something had been inserted into his anus had caused the police to treat the allegation as a possible sexual offence.

DG: 'Yes.'

HB: 'But nothing else about this allegation that is sexual?'

DG: 'I don't understand.'

HB: 'The first charge is indecent assault, but nothing else indecent about it?'

DG: 'I would say that inserting something into someone's bottom was indecent.'

HB: 'Because treated as a sexual offence, a log was created with the sexual offences team?'

DG: 'Yes.'

HB: 'That log has been lost?'

DG: 'Yes.'

HB: 'Because the defence asked for it?'

DG: 'Yes.'

Henry then asks how the log had been lost. Gadsby could not explain how he had lost the log and admitted responsibility for losing it. Henry then asked how another document, namely a diagram of the police station that Anqkar had drawn out, had got lost. Gadsby said that he had recalled seeing it but had no explanation of how this too had been lost.

HB: 'The documents found, Form 74 A, B and C, are documents that have long since ceased to be used by police?'

DG: 'I do not recall using them in my career.'

HB: 'They are documents which are peculiar to the time they were made. Document 74A – the arrest summons document – is it your understanding that this was the document that would be created when the case started?'

DG: 'That was my understanding from the information provided by Mr Hyde.'

HB: '74B is the result form. We can see here there are two officers recorded and it says under paragraph eighteen, about three quarters of the way down the page, he was convicted, pleaded guilty re: failing to appear, was convicted at Lambeth Juvenile Court and fined £5. Finally, the 74C at p. 6 of the bundle, this is the antecedence document, meaning the document relating to the circumstances of the individual, his name, address and date of birth. His home conditions and so on – we see that here. Going back to the 74A we have a 74A but it does not relate to the arrest on 31 October.'

DG: 'It doesn't appear to.'

HB: 'This relates to the arrest for failing to appear on 7 March?'
DG: 'Yes.'

Henry then moved on to the fingerprint form that the CPS provided as evidence that I arrested Anqkar on the night of the incident.

HB: 'This is another document that has not been included but was found by you, is it the fingerprint form?'
DG: 'Yes.'
HB: 'It appears to be the fingerprint form showing that his [Anqkar's] prints were taken at the time he was arrested for failing to appear.'
DG: 'The hole punch has taken the date out.'
HB: 'Look at the first page with the image of the prints on, it appears to say 5 March.'
DG: 'I can make an assumption that that is correct – it does say fail to appear.'

It was up to Henry, a barrister and not a police officer, to show Gadsby that the fingerprints the CPS had provided were for an offence of failing to appear in March 1987, not 31 October 1986.

HB: 'You have not found a 74A [arrest form] relating to 31 October's arrest?'
DG: 'It does not exist.'

HB: 'You have not found one. In order for Anqkar to be
charged and produced at court a Form 74A would have to
be produced.'
DG: 'I don't know. I don't know how accurately they were
produced.'
HB: 'Did you know it was the responsibility of the custody
officer to countersign this?'
DG: 'No.'

Henry then referred to Form 74B, a police form that is
completed after a result at court. This indicated that PC
Mady and I were at court when Anqkar was sentenced
in 1987.

HB: 'P. 10, officers present at court PC Virdi and PC Mady.
Have you made enquiries of PC Mady?'
DG: 'No.'
HB: 'Have you tried to find him?'
DG: 'No.'
HB: 'Why not?'
DG: 'I imagine we did not see the relevance of speaking
to that officer.'
HB: 'DC Markwick, speak to him?'
DG: 'He was spoken to over the course of the inquiry.'
HB: 'Was he?'
DG: 'I believe he was.'
HB: 'Is there a record of that?'
DG: 'If he was, it would be in the crime report.'

HB: 'It is not in the CRIS report.'

DG: 'It may be that I have misquoted, I would have to review the CRIS report. You have reviewed it and said it is not there. I have spoken to him in relation to your contact with him. I spoke to him prior to the statement being produced. He contacted us immediately following your contact with him.'

HB: 'Did you make a record of that?'

DG: 'I didn't make a record of the information.'

HB: 'It is quite important isn't it?'

DG: 'No, he did not provide any relevant information. He was more concerned with why he was being contacted.'

I couldn't believe that an investigations officer could not see the importance of contacting the only person directly connected to the October incident, and who was only contacted after Matt and I determined the importance of Markwick as a witness.

HB: 'Finally, the ASP – you made a number of enquires with officers about whether any of them had seen an ASP used at the time?'

DG: 'Yes.'

HB: 'And nobody had?'

DG: 'Correct.'

Henry then discussed something with Matt Foot. Matt passed him a note urging Henry to ask Gadsby about Anqkar's age.

HB: 'You had information from a very early stage that Mr Anqkar was sixteen at the time?'

DG: 'We had documentation that suggested that, yes.'

HB: 'Why was it that Mr Virdi was charged with an offence on a boy under the age of sixteen?'

DG: 'We did not cross reference the documentation with his account; we took account that he was fifteen.'

HB: 'The consequence of that is that there was a lot of publicity about the fact he had been charged with an indecent assault on a boy under sixteen?'

DG: 'Yes.'

[Gadbsy left the stand looking worried.]

Finally, it was my turn to give evidence. I left my glass cage and made my way to the witness stand. I affirmed, as I had always done during my years of police service. When I had first joined the Met, police officers had only been given two choices: swear on the bible or opt for affirmation. I had decided to opt for affirmation, as I am a person who has always respected all faiths and religions. Throughout my years of police service, I saw a number of people solemnly swear oaths while clutching their holy books – and then proceed to tell lies.

I shot a glance around the courtroom. My family were all inside, and this fact mattered to me a great deal. Gadsby was also there; he was sitting behind Evans and was with a female police officer. Gadsby was busy talking, and also seemed to be smirking. I had given evidence in court many times before over the years, but this time I felt angry. What was I doing here? Once again I had done nothing wrong; why was my family being put through this ordeal?

'I am fifty-six years old.' I told the court. 'I joined the Metropolitan Police in May 1982. I joined the crime squad, I believe, in 1985. I was there until April or May 1989.'

Then I read out my annual appraisal report for 1987, which stated:

'Appearance was assessed as very good, dresses to suit occasion. Consistently high standard of quality. Professional ability very good. Written work commensurate with present experience. Determined effort to be more outgoing. Described as a thorough investigator. Good standard. Does not overreact to situations. Very good working relationship with colleagues. Positive individual with potential to hold the rank of sergeant. Judgement good. Very reliable officer. Strong belief in own ability. Progressed to a good, above-average officer.'

I explained to the court that I had not been authorised to drive police vehicles, as this required an additional driving course that was never offered to me.

'PC Paul Mady was my partner at the time, I worked regularly with him. He was a police driver and I was not,' I said. 'I may have been out with Mr Makins on a couple of occasions. My long-term partners were PC Paul Mady and PC Derek True.'

I explained that after leaving the crime squad, I'd joined a squad at New Scotland Yard that had dealt with intelligence matters, and had remained there until 1993, when I was promoted to the rank of sergeant and transferred to the Ealing division. I outlined my experiences of racism in the police force during the 1980s.

'I was one of the very first officers from the Asian community; I was followed by two others,' I said. 'I suffered racism at the hands of other officers – uniform being damaged, name calling, things left in my tray. Some officers were very good. The south London community was very good; many of the residents accepted me and welcomed me, especially those from the ethnic minority communities.'

I turned to the time in 1998, when I had been investigated in relation to an incident in the Ealing division, after racist hate mail was distributed to police officers and civilian staff.

'There was a poor investigation into that. I was accused of having distributed this racist hate mail. I was actually arrested for it,' I said.

I explained that my arrest had happened soon after I'd questioned why a clash between five white and two Asian youths – which resulted in one youth being stabbed – had not been dealt with as a racist incident. I told the court I'd been dismissed from the police force by a 'kangaroo disciplinary board', but had been completely exonerated after taking my case to an employment tribunal. I had received compensation, been reinstated and given a public apology by Met Commissioner Sir John Stevens. I had then served in the Met as a detective sergeant until my retirement in May 2012.

I explained that when I was a police officer I had rarely carried handcuffs, although my partners had carried them. I also pointed out that we had not always handcuffed people, and that juveniles could not be handcuffed without a reason because they were vulnerable. I said I had not carried a truncheon when operating as a plain-clothes officer, and had not been carrying an ASP at the time of the alleged assault.

'I totally deny the allegations made against me,' I said. 'I deny that I called him [Anqkar] a "nigger". I never assaulted him in the back of the police van. I would never do such a thing.'

Anqkar's lawyer, Julian Evans, asked me whether it was possible that I had arrested Anqkar on 31 October 1986.

GV: 'I will say what I said in interview. Without my notes, my interview records and what happened in court I cannot comment. It shows that I was the arresting officer for the failing to appear.'

JE: 'Mr Makins gave evidence?'

GV: 'Yes.'

JE: 'He said that he was on duty with you in plain clothes on the evening of 31 October 1986; was he telling the truth about that?'

GV: 'I am very suspicious about that. Because if you look at the conviction certificate, Your Honour, at p. 2, this indicates to me that Harry Anqkar was arrested on 31 October. And the arresting officer there is DC Markwick, with a unique crime reference number in 1986. However, without looking at my notes, I cannot recall anything.'

JE: 'It does not say he [Markwick] was the arresting officer?'

I pointed to the document, and showed the court that the name of the informant or complainant was DC Markwick, who had been the arresting officer.

In regards to Anqkar's conviction for driving offences in 1987, the document showed me as the listed informant or complainant.

JE: 'Do you accept you did arrest him [Anqkar] in January 1987?'

GV: 'That is what it says here.'

JE: 'Do you have any recollection of it?'

GV: 'None whatsoever.'

I explained that my partner at the time of the alleged incident had been PC Mady, but said it was possible that Makins and I could have been working together as plain-clothes officers on 31 October 1986. Evans asked if I could recall having had any dealings with Anqkar before or prior to 31 October 1986.

GV: 'No, Mr Anqkar said so himself that it was the first time I met him.'

JE: 'Any dealings with him prior to January 1987?'

GV: 'Not to my knowledge.'

JE: 'In interview you were asked whether you alleged that there was a conspiracy in relation to this, and you answered yes?'

GV: 'Yes.'

JE: 'Is that still your opinion?'

GV: 'In interview, I was not given records. I asked for records. DC Gadsby responded: "For the fifth time there are
no records." In front of this court, there are records. I was
angry at the time. I was about to go into local politics and
this hurt my chances.'

JE: 'Is it still your case now that this is a conspiracy?'

GV: 'No, I think it is a case of incompetence.'

JE: 'So we can leave conspiracy aside?'

GV: 'For the moment.'

Evans asked me how I had got on with Makins. I answered
that I'd not particularly liked him, as he'd not been a 'hands-
on' person, and you'd had to push him to get him to do any
paperwork. I said no one had liked working with Makins, but
that if I was told to work with him then I did so.

JE: 'And you suspected him of being racist to you?'

GV: 'Yes.'

JE: 'Is that still your suspicion?'

GV: 'As soon as he left, hate mail that I had received and
was being put in my tray stopped.'

Evans suggested that Makins had never behaved to me in a
racist manner. But I pointed out to him that Makins had told
me he'd left the crime squad because he didn't like working
in south London, as there were too many black people there.

JE: 'You didn't mention that in interview?'

GV: 'I wasn't asked.'

Evans asked me if I could remember ever giving information about Anqkar to any of my police colleagues. I said I had no recollection of ever having done this.

JE: 'He [Anqkar] was someone of interest to the crime squad?'
GV: 'According to Mr Makins.'

Evans turned to the culture of policing in Britain in the 1980s, and asked me how it compared to the culture of modern-day policing. I told him that some things had not changed. Racism remained rife, and there were still many 'stop and search' incidents.

JE: 'White officers beating up black prisoners; that was happening then?'
GV: 'Yes, it was.'

Evans turned to documents concerning an arrest of Anqkar.

JE: 'P. 9, you were the arresting officer of Mr Anqkar for driving matters, how did that come about?'
GV: 'Without looking at records, I could not say. I gave a couple of examples of how it would happen, this could be one of those.'
JE: 'You were the arresting officer?'
GV: 'Yes. My case, it says here.'

JE: 'Were you looking for Mr Anqkar?'
GV: 'Not at all.'

Evans continued to push for an explanation of why I would have arrested Anqkar for the driving offences. He kept insinuating that this arrest followed on from me searching for Anqkar. I continued to assert that I was not looking for him, as I did not know Anqkar.

> JE: 'Could Mr Makins be right about you being on duty with him?'
> GV: 'The only arrest I remember with Mr Makins is we arrested two people for robbery and he messed up the identification procedure and when we got back to the police station he was severely reprimanded.'

Evans then asked me how I would deal with people resisting arrest. I said that it depended on the situation and circumstances; for example, if someone was running, I would try to catch them. He then asked me about usage of old-style handcuffs with a chain.

I explained that the rules for using handcuffs at the time were strict, and such usage had to be justified and explained to the custody sergeant. Evans's line of questioning was very much directed at getting me to admit that I would have used handcuffs when making routine arrests of suspects in connection with alleged robberies or possession of a knife.

Evans then wanted to know about police informants, as

Anqkar had claimed to be one. I told Evans that this was impossible as Anqkar had been a juvenile, and juveniles were
not allowed to become police informants.

Evans was not getting what he wanted, but continued to
press me about approaching Anqkar as a possible informant.

JE: 'Did you approach juveniles?'
GV: 'No, you did not do that, the rules were very strict.'
JE: 'What were the rules in 1986?'
GV: 'You could not speak to them without an appropriate
adult being present.'
JE: 'Mr Makins said it was part of the job.'

Evans then turned to Anqkar's conviction certificate related to
carrying an offensive weapon and failing to appear in court. He
asked if I had attended court in respect of this matter. I said I had.

JE: 'You had taken over as the officer in the case?'
GV: 'Yes, because DC Markwick had left by that point.'
JE: 'How does his [Markwick] name appear on the convic-
tion certificate?'
GV: 'Let me clarify. Mr Anqkar has been arrested in
October 1987 according to this document [conviction
certificate] of DC Markwick's. From this paperwork, the
arrest is not even mine.'
JE: '1986?'
GV: 'Yes, sorry. DC Markwick has left Battersea. Mr Anqkar
has then failed to attend court and I have arrested him [in

March 1987] and have become the officer in the case. An officer cannot be expected to be the officer in the case when they have left.'

JE: 'You are officer in the case for the whole case?'

I knew Evans was trying his hardest to get me to say that I had been the officer for the whole case, but this was impossible because Markwick had been involved in the October 1986 arrest.

JE: 'Any recollection of giving evidence of the possession of offensive weapon charge?'

GV: 'I have no recollection. This is a lock knife, you would have to withdraw it from the property store and I do not recall doing that. Because I am dealing with the fail to appear which he pleaded guilty to I probably did not give evidence.'

JE: 'You are the officer who arrested Mr Anqkar for failing to appear?'

GV: 'Yes.'

JE: 'What was the failing to appear for?'

GV: 'For the original offence of possession of an offensive weapon.'

JE: 'Does this jog your memory of involvement in the possession of offensive weapon arrest?'

GV: 'No, no, no. I am not making myself clear. Someone has not appeared at court. Say for example someone is due in court in London and is arrested in Birmingham. The officer in Birmingham would do this form. It is a different crime reference number.'

JE: 'Jog your memory as to whether he having failed to attend on that occasion you were looking for him?'

GV: 'Without looking at papers, I do not know; he might have handed himself in at the police station.'

JE: 'Arrested him also for driving matters?'

GV: 'It would appear so.'

JE: 'A number of times over this relatively short period you had dealings with Mr Anqkar?'

GV: 'As with a number of other people.'

JE: 'Suggest that you were on duty with PC Makins on 31 October?'

I was getting frustrated. The paperwork clearly stated that I had been at the court with Mady in 1987, but Evans was continuing to try and make a link with Makins. I relayed my frustration to Evans.

GV: 'I come back to the same point that we [Mady and I] went to court and they heard the evidence and he was convicted. Are you having a retrial here? It is amazing that all the paperwork from 1986 has disappeared, but here is a document from 1987 that has been linked.'

JE: 'Disappearing paperwork: is that part of a conspiracy as well?'

At this point, my daughter, Kesar, stormed out of the court-room. Evans continued to press me.

JE: 'I suggest that you did arrest him [Anqkar] and put him into handcuffs. I suggest you did ask him his name and slap him across the face and say: 'What kind of name is that for a nigger?'... grabbed the handcuffs and swung him around the van, inserted something into his bottom ... that thing was a collapsible truncheon...'

I firmly pointed out that ASPs had not been available until a decade after the alleged incident. 'I find it very amazing that you are asking me these questions when DC Gadsby goes to court and gives false information about this boy [Anqkar] being under sixteen, he messes up again ... he went to court again and got it wrong again, again said he was under six- teen. That is proven evidence of him lying to the court.'

Evans cut me short and put the allegations to me again. I calmed myself down and finished by stating that I had sat on a Youth Justice Panel and had tried to steer young people away from crime. I was not the person Evans was making me out to be.

Then it was Henry's turn to re-examine me. He asked whether I had been successful in the local council elections.

'Yes, despite the bad publicity given by DC Gadsby and his false allegations. The local people trusted me and they elected me.'

I felt that I had said my bit. The prosecution were not seek- ing the truth; all they were concerned about was getting a conviction by trying to trap me into saying something that

I had not done. I felt this was reflected in Evans's line of questioning – he kept asking the same questions in different ways, and not once did he provide a single piece of evidence that linked me to Anqkar on 31 October 1986, apart from Anqkar's and Makins's accounts.

A number of witness statements concerning my character were then read out to the court. The first was from Graham Markwick, who had worked at the Met until retiring in 1998 after thirty-two years. Graham had mentored me and had worked alongside me in two of my police postings. In his statement, he said that I was the last person he would have expected to be violent. He also said he never saw me with an ASP.

The second statement was from Dr Richard Stone OBE, who was part of the 1997/99 Home Office inquiry into the murder of Stephen Lawrence. Dr Stone said my submission to the inquiry panel had confirmed that some 'dreadful weaknesses' of the Stephen Lawrence investigation had also clearly occurred in other cases. He said my submission had been one of the first to point the inquiry in the direction of its final conclusion, that 'institutional racism' was not confined to the Stephen Lawrence case. Dr Stone described me as 'courteous, intelligent and thoughtful'.

The statement from Hayes and Harlington MP, John McDonnell, revealed that he had known me for nearly twenty years. He said I was an active and highly respected member of the community, and was 'honest, responsible and caring'. He said I showed 'good judgement and wise decision making', and he trusted me 'implicitly'.

The final statement was from journalist and broadcaster Baron Singh of Wimbledon, who said he had advised, or been a member of, the Commission for Racial Equality and the Home Secretary's Advisory Council on Race Relations. Baron Singh said he was aware I had been prominent in fighting racism in the Metropolitan Police, and that this had resulted in a degree of animosity towards me. He said I had been actively involved with the Sikh community for many years and had no reason to doubt my character or integrity.

Prosecutor Julian Evans then rose to make his closing argument, which was much the same as the one he made at the opening of the trial. Then it was Henry's turn to stand up and make his closing speech.

Henry pointed out that there were obvious cracks in the prosecution's case. The revelations of sexual abuse by TV star Jimmy Savile had reminded those working in the criminal justice system that complaints of malpractice against people in authority had to be taken seriously, but the Savile revelations also risked creating a bandwagon for people with ancient grudges. He addressed the court: 'And, worse, it creates the possibility that the unscrupulous exploit public sympathy for the victims of historic abuse for their own financial objectives.'

He stated that the prosecution had relied on two witnesses, Anqkar and Makins. But Makins had flatly contradicted much of Anqkar's evidence. 'Mr Makins's evidence on its own, and taken at its highest, does not prove that Gurpal

Virdi is guilty of the serious offence of misconduct in a public office, let alone the offence of indecent assault.'

Henry admitted that I was an angry man, but he explained that I had a good reason to be angry:

> Not only does he have first-hand experience as a victim of racist conduct, he was quite outrageously dismissed on groundless charges which were roundly rejected by an employment tribunal. He courageously returned to work in the Met, in order, as he told Dr Stone, to change the police for the better. For years he has had to battle against prejudice and a hostile working environment.
>
> So you might have thought that when someone came forward to accuse him of a horrendous racist attack that he, of all people, would have been entitled to have the allegation investigated by the police thoroughly and conscientiously. You might have thought that the police and the Department of Professional Standards would have learnt the lessons of the past. Not a bit of it. He has been treated to a thoroughly unprofessional and shoddy investigation.

Henry told the jury they did not have to conclude that there had been a conspiracy to frame me in order to acquit me, but he added that a question did hang over the case. 'Why on earth was Gurpal Virdi charged with these very serious criminal offences, when it must have been perfectly obvious to anyone investigating these allegations that Anqkar was a witness who simply could not be believed?'

Arguing that perhaps Anqkar's allegations had been financially motivated, Henry told the court: 'He [Anqkar] is quite
clearly driven by financial considerations. He is after money
and thinks Mr Virdi is worth a few pennies. Sadly, he has
clearly prevailed on both his father and his partner, Linda
Taylor, to support his lies.'

Henry went on to explain that it was 'wholly unsafe' for
the jury to rely on a single word Anqkar had said. Anqkar
had told ten clear lies.

THE TEN LIES

Firstly, he told you that he had informed his solicitor about
what had happened, but she hadn't wanted to pursue it. He
said the solicitor said there weren't interview tapes. You
didn't have tapes then; it was before interviews were taped.

Secondly, he said he told the court at the time and the
magistrates told him to shut up. The point is that he was
asked that question by PC Newton in the video interview.
He said "no". That's a second lie.

Thirdly is the clearest example, one that really throws
into question why this case was brought – the allegation
about the ASP. He was clear in his interviews that a collapsible truncheon had been inserted into his anus. The
prosecution tried to suggest Mr Virdi may have had another object. This has gone nowhere. The obvious problem
is that Mr Virdi said he had nothing.

Henry said Anqkar had been asked again, in August 2014, whether it was a collapsible truncheon and had even gone so far as to say that he had seen not only me, but also another officer, with an ASP. This had been an 'obvious, clear and demonstrable lie,' Henry stated.

Continuing to list Anqkar's inconsistencies, Henry stated:

Fourthly, he told you that he was harassed by Gurpal Virdi, who picked him up and drove him around in his car. Mr Virdi wasn't a police driver. When this was pointed out to him [Anqkar], he reached for the water and tried to change his evidence. He said he wasn't driving. There was someone else in the car. This is a dishonest witness.

Fifthly, he lied about saying he was fifteen – he gave his date of birth; he would have known he was sixteen at the time. He told officers he was fifteen, he said: 'I'm going to tell my dad about this when I'm interviewed.' There hadn't been a word about that previously. He volunteered that at the first time: a clear embellishment which was a lie.

Anqkar's sixth lie involved his address, Henry told the jury. Anqkar had said that he was living in Brussels Road with his parents at the time, but then moved to Effra Road, Brixton, because I was harassing him.

Henry explained that 'he was clear in interviews. He told Doherty he was homeless then went to live with his brother in Effra Road. He lied about where he was living. The reason was because if he was living in Effra Road, he wouldn't have a reason for being in Plough Road.'

Anqkar's seventh lie concerned the knife he had used. 'He said it was a Stanley knife,' Henry reminded the jury. 'This is a good example of why having documents would assist. Despite the suggestion by DC Gadsby that a Stanley knife could be confused with a lock knife, it is perfectly clear that you cannot confuse a lock knife with a Stanley knife. Why does he say Stanley knife? – to support the claim that he was on youth work experience at the time.'

Henry asserted that Anqkar had told his eighth lie when he was asked if he wanted to sue the police. Anqkar had at first claimed that he was not interested in suing the police, but after being confronted over his taped phone conversation with Michael Doherty, when Anqkar had said: 'Oh God yes! I definitely want to sue the police,' had then admitted that this had been his intention.

His ninth lie involved his statement to the psychotherapist about the injury to his wrists.

'He made no mention of report to the psychotherapist that he had long-term nerve damage to his wrists,' Henry told the court.

Anqkar's tenth lie concerned his marriage. He had lied about this because he had not known he was going to be asked about it, Henry said.

'Are you ever going to see a clearer example of perjury in a criminal case? This is a witness who has perjured himself serially in giving evidence,' Henry told the court.

'Everything we know about Gurpal Virdi makes it wholly improbable that he would have behaved in the way described by Anqkar – a savage, unprovoked racist attack.'

Henry said that I had a history of confronting racist conduct at not inconsiderable personal cost. He pointed out that my report to the Stephen Lawrence inquiry had specifically made the point that black people were more likely to be stopped and charged. Henry concluded that it was inconceivable that I could have acted in the manner that Anqkar had claimed I had acted.

CHAPTER 16

THE VERDICT

JUDGE GOYMER'S ADDRESS

Members of the jury, on this count of misconduct in a public office, there are two questions that you must decide. Firstly, did the defendant do the acts alleged? Secondly, if he did, do they amount to misconduct in public office? Misconduct in public office must be more than just using excessive force to restrain a prisoner or being a bit heavy-handed when dealing with him. There is, of course, no excuse for police officers to use racist language but you still have to decide whether even that is serious enough to amount to the offence…

Let's turn from misconduct in public office to the other count on the indictment. That is the count of indecent assault. What do the prosecution have to prove for indecent assault? The thing they of course have to prove is that Mr Anqkar is a male person; well, there is no dispute about that.

What is an indecent assault? An indecent assault is any assault accompanied by circumstances of indecency which is really saying the same thing in different words. So, let's break it down in its component parts and see what it involves. An assault is deliberate and unlawful physical contact with another person. Deliberate means that it was not done accidentally or even carelessly. Unlawful means that it was not done with the consent of the other person. What is indecent is for you to decide, not me. You must judge this by applying current standards of behaviour and decency and you must ask this question: is what was done so offensive to current standards of decency and privacy that it should be classed as indecent? Now, it is for you and not me to say what is indecent. You may, however, think that if you are sure the defendant did do what it is alleged with the baton, then you will also conclude that it was indecent. The defendant must know that his conduct is indecent; he must intend to act indecently. Again, if you are sure that he did do what is alleged, you would not have any difficulty on that.

Just a word or two about consent. Any touching of the complainant, that is, Mr Anqkar, must be done without his consent. As a matter of law, the prosecution has to prove that he did not consent. Mr Anqkar told you, if not in as many words, clearly implied in his evidence, that he did not consent to being touched in that way and that he did nothing to cause the defendant to believe that he was consenting to it. His evidence on this point has never been challenged. The defendant, for his part, has not said that he did believe Mr Anqkar was consenting to whatever was done, therefore, if you are sure that he did assault him and that it was indecent, you are entitled to conclude without any further evidence that Mr Anqkar did not consent to it and that the defendant did not believe that he was consenting. That is for you to decide and not me ... In this case you are going to have to assess the evidence of Mr Anqkar very carefully in order to decide whether the prosecution have proved the case against the defendant. By its very nature, sexual activity rarely, if ever, takes place in front of witnesses. You do of course know that in this case there is a witness present, PC Makins, the other officer, but he did not claim to see anything of an indecent nature happen. For this reason, therefore, you must bear in mind that it is relatively easy to make an allegation of sexual misbehaviour and it is equally difficult for a defendant to refute or disprove it.

False allegations may be made for a whole variety of reasons, sometimes for no obvious reason at all. Here, the reason is said to be that Mr Anqkar is hoping to get compensation in a civil court. When you therefore consider his evidence, you should look to see whether there is any other evidence which supports what Mr Anqkar has told you. That evidence must be independent of what Mr Anqkar has told you, so it follows that a complaint that is made to any other person at any other time whenever it was cannot be supporting evidence, because it does not come from another source. Until he made an official complaint to the police in March of 2013, there was no complaint made to any independent person as opposed to a member of his family. In any event, it appears that it was first mentioned to anybody at least five years and possibly seven years after the event.

My task is to point out to you what can and, perhaps more importantly, what cannot be supporting evidence. I have to tell you there is no independent supporting evidence for what Mr Anqkar has told you. There is no eyewitness to it, there is no medical evidence, there is no DNA. There is no evidence of the defendant being found in possession of a truncheon of the type described. It is not essential for there to be supporting evidence. You are entitled to accept the complainant's evidence without it, there is no rule of law which says you cannot be sure when it is just one person's word against another. If it is just one person's word against another, this is simply something you have to take into account in deciding whether you are sure. You have also heard that long after this alleged incident Mr Anqkar made a complaint to members of his family, much later than that to the police. It is not evidence as to what actually happened between him and the defendant for obvious reasons. None of these witnesses were present and they did not see what happened between them…

Let me go on to deal with another matter of law and that is the question of good character. This defendant, as you know, is a man, now fifty-six years of age, and of good character with no previous convictions or cautions at all recorded against him. In addition, you have heard evidence of his good character, not just in that negative sense but in a positive sense from statements made by other witnesses which were read to you. That he was a highly professional officer who took his work seriously and, indeed, took active steps to combat racism in the Metropolitan Police and to promote good community relations. What is the effect of good character when it is raised in a criminal trial? It cannot in the nature of things be a complete defence, but it is important and you must take it into account in these two ways.

Firstly, the defendant has given evidence from the witness box. His good character supports his credibility as a witness. What that means is that it makes him more believable. You must take this into account when deciding whether you believe his evidence or think that it may be true. Secondly, his good character affects the likelihood of his having committed the offences. The fact is that he has both reached the age that he has and has done so without committing any offence. This means that it is less likely he has committed the offences for which he is on trial. It is not impossible but it is less likely and you must also take into account when deciding whether the prosecution have made you sure that he is guilty. You must also take into account a third aspect of good character which arises from the delay in this case. The events with which we are concerned happened a very long time ago. During all the years that have intervened, the defendant has come into contact with a variety of people. Yet, nobody else has made allegations of this kind against him.

That is good character but what about bad character? You have heard the defendant is a man of good character and by contrast, you have heard Mr Anqkar has previous criminal convictions. He was of course convicted of having an offensive weapon all those years ago in 1987. You also know that in 2004 he was convicted of a bankruptcy offence of making a transfer of property to his partner in order to defeat any claim by his creditors. Why have you heard about these and how can they help you to decide the case? They are not put forward just gratuitously to smear or discredit him, they are put forward for good reasons. One of the questions which may arise is whether he was telling the truth about the circumstances in which he came to be arrested.

Mr Anqkar said that he was carrying a Stanley knife as one of the tools of his trade when he was on work experience. The court record, which is before you suggest it is a lock knife which is quite different. A person with criminal convictions may be less likely to tell the truth, but does not mean he is incapable of ever telling the truth or has lost all right to ever be believed. It may or may not help you on the question of whether Mr Anqkar is an honest witness, who is trying to tell the truth and can be relied on. It is a matter for you and for you alone to decide if this evidence of his bad character helps you at all and, if so, how much it helps you.

I have mentioned something about delay, so let's look at the question of delay. In this case the events with which you are concerned about happened a very long time ago; in 1986, that is now twenty-nine years ago. If you just pause to reflect on events, which have happened in your own personal lives or on public events in the outside world, then you will realise. There are, for example, people who were born after that date who probably now have children of their own. It just gives you some idea how long a time has gone by. What is the importance of delay; how does it affect the case?

Delay affects the memory of witnesses, as we all know. They may not have had cause to remember events at the time and, so, the details may have faded from their memory. Even when they can or, more importantly, they think that they can remember the details, the memory can play tricks on them and can mean that what they believe to be their clear recollection is totally distorted and inaccurate. Again, you probably have experience of that in your own lives. Perhaps of somebody saying to you that they are convinced they were present at a particular event, and then it happens you produce a photograph, it is clear that they were not present at that event. That is how the memory plays tricks over that period of time. People can have fixed idea in their own minds about how events were and that may be completely different from reality. This can affect witnesses on both sides, but it is the prosecution who must prove the defendant's guilt, not the defendant who must prove his innocence.

There is a delay, not only in the events themselves, but in reporting them to the authorities for investigation. The investigation did not get underway until March 2013 and that, if my arithmetic is correct, would even then be twenty-six years after the events. This puts the defendant at a serious disadvantage in trying to defend himself against these charges. He of course has to prove nothing because it is always for the prosecution to prove that he is guilty. A defendant is always entitled to say to the prosecution: 'Well, if you say I am guilty, you prove it.' Many defendants may want to put forward a positive case that actually disproves their guilt or even proves their innocence. Delay can deprive a defendant of this opportunity. Why is that?

Firstly, witnesses who could help his case have disappeared or become untraceable. If they can be found, they are no longer able to remember events after this long lapse of time. One example of a witness who has not been traced in this case is the driver of the police van. There were various versions of his name given, but he has never been traced, so that is one witness, that is an example of it. The second way in which delay can deprive the defendant of that opportunity is that documents which could help by providing a contemporaneous record of events or the names of people who were present and might remember them have been lost through the passage of time. Alternatively, they have been destroyed because nobody at the time thought that they might still be important or that there could ever have been any further use for them in the future. A lot of documents relating to the court proceedings are lost or destroyed. You only have the basics in the court record. You must therefore remember the difficulty that the defendant faces on that.

There is one aspect of delay and what I might call 'Delay: Part One', there is another direction on delay which I will call 'Delay: Part Two'. Delay in reporting an allegation is obviously something that you must consider. Experience does show that people will react differently to the trauma of an alleged sexual assault and there is no one classic response. There are two different ways of looking at it. On the one hand, a complaint that is made very soon after the alleged incident is more likely to be true because there has been less time to think up a false story or to be persuaded that apparently, innocent events have a more sinister meaning. On the other hand, it does not necessarily follow that a delayed complaint is a false one. People in those situations may, for a whole variety of reasons, be unwilling to complain at the time. They may feel embarrassed to talk about such things; they may fear that they would not be believed if they do speak out or that they may be blamed for what happened. People will, of course, feel a sense of humiliation at what happened to them, if that happened to them it may be they are reluctant to talk. So, you must bear all those things in mind. It does not automatically follow that a delayed complaint is a false one, any more than it follows a prompt complaint is a true one.

In recent years, particularly, we have had a lot of experience in these courts of adults reporting, years later, things they say happened to them when they were children. The children in each case has to make up their own mind as to whether they are sure these things did happen. It is a

matter for you to decide, not me, if the question of delay
helps you at all. If so, how much. Does it help you to decide
the question of whether you are sure Mr Anqkar has told
the truth and given a reliable account of what happened…

Talking about the complainant, let me go on to say
something else. You must be very careful not to use the
word 'victim'. It is a word that people use far too much
these days. The prosecution still has to prove that the defendant is guilty. If you use that word, it can make you
think that the defendant is automatically guilty. The danger
is then of thinking that what the prosecution still have to
prove has already been approved. That is why I always use
the neutral word 'complainant'. Nobody is a victim unless
and until it is proved that a crime has been committed.
Remember, a person wrongly or falsely accused of a crime
is just as much a victim. Sometimes people who claim to
be the victims of crime do not always tell the whole truth.
Sometimes, they give an account which even if it is honest
is not accurate or reliable. I am not saying this happens all
the time, but you must always consider it, that is why we
have juries for; to decide what is and what is not reliable.

It may be that one of the questions you will ask yourselves; perhaps one posed by the prosecution is, well, why
should Mr Anqkar have gone through all this trouble to
make him persist in a false accusation? That is something
you may wish to consider. On the other hand, you must remember that if a person does make a false allegation then,
in a sense, he has gone down a road from which there is no

turning back because the momentum of the investigation will carry him along even if he stops to think, there are obvious dangers in turning back. Sometimes, people who have made false allegations think it is better to carry on and be disbelieved and be able to claim thereafter that they are the victims of some miscarriage of justice. It is not helpful in this case to say that one side or other must be lying because this will bring emotion into the case. You are entitled to ask the question; what reason is there for Mr Anqkar to make this up. Do not fall into the trap of thinking that the defendant has to produce a reason why he has done this. Remember, as I have said to you several times; the burden of proof is always on the prosecution to make you sure the defendant is guilty. You must ask yourselves whether the prosecution has made you sure that there is no reason for Mr Anqkar to make this up, or even any reason why he may have done so. If you are sure that you can rule out this possibility, this may, but not automatically, lead to the conclusion that the prosecution has proved the case. You have to consider whether he has given you an honest account of what happened. In other words, is he trying to tell the truth? If you think that he is not or may not even be trying to tell you the truth, that is the end of the case of this defendant and you would find him not guilty. If you are sure that he is trying to tell the truth, you are still faced with the further and possibly more difficult question of whether his account is reliable and accurate. It is therefore important for his evidence to be not only honest but reliable.

Members of the jury, let's turn now to look at the evidence in the case … In doing so, what I am going to do is not just to read out every word of evidence you have heard, I am going to remind you at stages about some of the ways in which some evidence is at variance between the witnesses and also some of the things which are not present in this case.

Mr Anqkar told you that it was in March 2013 that he made a statement about what had happened to him after his arrest of possessing an offensive weapon when he was aged sixteen, on 31 October 1986. He said the so-called weapon was a Stanley knife. You have the point but you will have to consider is his evidence reliable on that because the court record suggests that it was a lock knife that was something different. He told you about the altercation he had with a man called 'Denzel' and then this; when he was in Plough Road he attracted the attention of two men in plain clothes who turned out to be police officers and, indeed, none other than the defendant and PC Makins as he then was. Mr Anqkar had not seen either of them before. He got to realise that the defendant went by the name of 'George', his first name is Gurpal but he may have been, because his colleagues used the English name of 'George'.

He said that George and Tom, that is Mr Makins, were in the back of a white van, there is some discrepancy as to whether Mr Makins did go and speak to Denzel or not. You will have to make up your mind of whether that is important. He described how George was holding him by his arm and that the van he was put inside was a white Sherpa, a transit-size van. In those days, police vans had just two benches on either side, you could stand up in it, but not probably high, and the lighting was not very good. There was no holding area inside the van. According to Mr Anqkar, it started with the defendant asking his name and handcuffing him. There may be an issue, which you have to decide, as to whether he was handcuffed or not. George asked him what his name was; he said Harry Anqkar. According to Mr Anqkar, the defendant smacked him across the face by a downward movement and then after the racist remark, 'What kind of name is that for a fucking nigger?' then he said it escalated. He started beating, punching and kicking and trying to get him into a headlock. He tried to grab him around the head and you will remember he said that during the course of the fight he was beaten by the defendant. He started hitting every part of the inside of the van, except the roof. He said: 'George was swinging me with the handcuffs and Tom got out of the way.' According to him, Tom was screaming out at George to get off him. 'Get off him, George, you're fucking killing him. Why are you behaving like this?'

According to Mr Anqkar, the entreaties of Mr Makins had no effect on him. In the end, he ended up on the floor in a foetal position and then he said: 'I felt a sharp pain up my backside. I realised he was shoving something into my anus. I thought it was his thumb. It was continuous; it went on for about ten seconds. I was in a lot of pain and all

I could do was kick my legs out. My lower clothing was a pair of shell bottoms.'

Some of you probably remember the 1980s, people wore shell suits, these thin tracksuits made of nylon. That is what he was wearing at the time and said the baton was pushed through the shell bottoms and the underpants he was wearing. He said that he saw an object in his hand while he was in the van, kicking the van doors open. Tom, that is PC Makins, banged on the partition for the van to stop. The van stopped and do you remember Mr Anqkar described it – because it was night of course, it was about 6.30 p.m. – that there was street light and he thought George was caught like a rabbit in the headlights of a car. He said this was a small collapsible truncheon. It was black in colour, it was metal, like the handle of a golf club, about ten inches long. He said that he had seen these on TV before. He was then taken to the police station and says he came up with this remark: "I can't believe you've done that to a fifteen-year-old. I wasn't actually fifteen at the time. I was sixteen." One of them, that's George, said: "Well, what's your fucking date of birth then?"'

Let's just remember this, it was 31 October 1986 and Mr Anqkar's date of birth is 29 August 1970 and so he was then two months beyond his sixteenth birthday. Was it a mistake on his part or may it have been a lie? Why was it a lie if he said that? You will of course remember the criticism is made by the defence that the defendant was initially charged with indecent assault on somebody under sixteen and when it was known or ought to have been known at the time, Mr Anqkar was sixteen years of age.

He then described how he was eventually released from the police station. He was not interviewed and later he appeared in court. He said that when he went downstairs, he met his stepfather and according to Mr Anqkar, he told his stepfather: 'They've beaten me up really badly and he stuck his truncheon up my ass.' He said, 'The way my dad (as he referred to him) reacted, he didn't believe what I'd said.' Then he went on to deal with occasions when he said he was subsequently harassed by the defendant who arrested him for nothing more than standing outside a car, at the bottom of the road and that ended up with him somehow being convicted of driving without a license or insurance. He said George would drive around in his car, tapping his truncheon on the window and making faces at him, as though to imply 'You and I both know what the truncheon means.' Later on, he told you about how his life moved on from there, how he met his current partner, Linda Taylor, and a good many years after they had got together, he told her about the assault on the truncheon.

Let's just pause there, members of the jury, because there are certain things you will have to consider about Mr Anqkar's evidence. First of all, let's look at the baton. There is independent evidence that no baton of this type, the extendable one, was issued to the Metropolitan Police before the 1990s. You have also heard that the manufacturer in the United States, although it had manufactured it since 1978, did not export them outside that country until a decade later in 1987. The evidence that was read to you of Mr Markwick, now retired, who was a former supervising detective constable and who knew the defendant confirmed this. Mr Markwick also said that he never saw the defendant or any other crime squad officer with one. It is also important to remind you when we look at the evidence of Mr Makins. Mr Makins did not see the defendant in possession of a baton at any time. You will remember the defendant and Mr Makins and, indeed, I think Mr Markwick made this point about the baton. These were officers who were involved in plain-clothed duties. In order to carry out their plain-clothed duties effectively, they had to dress in a way which would make them look just part of the ordinary crowd in the street.

They therefore did not carry these batons because it would simply become obvious that they were carrying a baton in their pocket and that would give them away to any potential criminal as police officers. You will therefore have to bear that point in mind. Mr Anqkar was asked about the injuries which he had because he said that from the assault he was dragged around with the handcuffs on, he ended up with what looked like metal burn marks on his wrists. He did not show those to the custody sergeant at the police station. He said he did not think the custody officer would listen to him. Another thing which he is criticised for and it is said he came out with for the first time, is that at the time of the incident he told police that he was

fifteen years old, which of course was not true, and that
when he was interviewed, he would tell everybody about
what had happened. We know he was not interviewed and
he agreed when he was cross examined by Mr Blaxland
that this was the first time he had mentioned this to anybody that he said this.

   You will have to ask yourselves; is that a case of remembering it because nobody asked him about it before? Is it
perhaps something he has made up as he was going along?
He was then asked about any injuries and he said that not
only did he not show the injuries to the custody officer;
he did not seek any medical assistance. He never went to
a doctor about the injuries which he had. He described
the after effects of it and said he did not have any cuts or
damage to his clothing, visible injuries. He said he felt sore
afterwards from the use of the baton. He said for a week it
hurt to go to the toilet but he did not suffer from bleeding
and he did not go to the doctor. He came out with that
detail about his pants being soiled and said well, that was
just something unpleasant and embarrassing which he did
not really want to mention to anybody. Again, you must
consider all that. He was also asked about an interview he
had and things he said to other police officers who interviewed him, things which he had not added but mentioned
later. You will bear that in mind. Let us look now, if we may,
members of the jury, at the evidence of Mr Makins.

   He was a police constable in the Metropolitan Police
from 1981 to 1987. He then left the Metropolitan Police, I

think, for personal or family reasons and joined the police in Guernsey where he continued the rest of his police career from May 1987 until 2013, when he returned with the rank of uniformed inspector. He said that he knew the defendant quite well, they were both on the crime squad and he said that he knew Mr Anqkar quite well. He described him as a prominent nominal or target, that is to say somebody the police were interested in because he was suspected of being involved in street crime. You will remember the point that was made about why Mr Anqkar was there and what he said about his arrest. He said that he saw Mr Anqkar sometime between 5.30 p.m. and 7.00 p.m. in the area. He was looking for him proactively but he did not actually catch him in the act of committing any crime. In due course, he was arrested for something at least but then when he was found in possession of the knife, he was arrested for having an offensive weapon. Mr Makins described going into the van, he could not quite remember the name of the driver and thought it was Dave Wilder or Wildbore or some name like that; anyway, he has never been traced. He said the lighting was not good inside the van and it was a restricted area. He was sat behind the driver and then as regards events happening he said: 'I can't recall exactly what he said but I recall some comments about arresting him.'

You will, of course, remember that Mr Makins is not relying on notes which he made at the time, he is having to give this account from memory many years later when he may not necessarily have had any particular reason for remembering what was, in other circumstances, a fairly routine arrest. He said that he saw Mr Anqkar stand up and then the defendant grabbed him. They were not big punches or kicks, but it was pure force and he wrestled him with physical force. It was quite a small, confined space. These were not big punches, not hay makers and they were not run-ups; he did not run up to him and kick him, it was enough force to think he was going over the top. 'More than I thought was enough force to restrain him.'

Be careful about that, members of the jury, because Mr Makins may be acting with hindsight, looking back on events many years later. You will also remember that he went on to say, 'I thought he was going over the top. It went on for a few seconds before I intervened. My view was that it was excessive force being used to detain a youth of this age who was in a police van and posing no threats.' He said they were exchanging insults but he could not recall the exact words.

'I can't recall if Mr Anqkar remained standing. It's a small area, it was a bit like a broom cupboard. But I never saw the defendant holding anything. I never saw him assault Mr Anqkar in any way with a baton. I didn't see any injury.' Not only that, Mr Makins said that he never made any kind of report to the custody sergeant or to any other officer, that he was concerned about the way in which the defendant had dealt with that situation. What he did confirm was that he, himself, very rarely carried a truncheon.

There were the old-fashioned, wooden truncheons which were generally carried by uniformed officers who had special pockets on their uniforms for them but not by plain-clothed officers.

'I never saw any extendable batons. I never saw any member of the crime squad in possession of them at any time in either uniform or plain clothes and I never saw the defendant in possession of any unauthorised equipment.'

Something which was also confirmed by the statement of Mr Markwick that was read out to you. He said that he could not say whether he saw the defendant punching or kicking him. It was very difficult going back all those number of years and:

'If somebody stands up, the first thing you do is you stand up and stop a prisoner getting out of control. Started with verbal aggression. He, that is, Mr Anqkar, was a bit of a gobby teenager and things can happen quite quickly; I don't recall him using any kind of racist remark like that. I can't recall the exact words used. I can't recall him hitting Mr Anqkar across the face or pulling him around by hand-cuffs to hand. For a prisoner to kick the van doors open is not that unusual. He didn't appear to have any injuries and I didn't see anything happen that could have caused injuries. I would describe it as having been excessively manhandled. I could have brought it to the notice of my supervisors if I wanted to press it, I suppose, but I didn't.'

You then heard evidence from Mr Sautelabaap, Mr Anqkar's stepfather. He said that Mr Anqkar did not tell him anything about what happened at the time of arrest, 'I didn't want to know.' He said that he did tell the police that Harry, that is his stepson, did not like Indians and 'much more recently, Harry had told me that he'd been assaulted by a police officer and had a baton up his bottom'. That seems to have been around 2007, so that is something in the order of twenty years after the event.

Mr Anqkar's partner, Ms Taylor, gave evidence that some years, a couple of years after their relationship had started which was in the late '80s, round about 1988, he said that he had been assaulted when he had been arrested. She just thought that there was nothing significant in that, that perhaps he was just being a bit of a bad boy at the time. Later, probably about five years after the relationship started, possibly longer than that, he mentioned for the first time that the policeman, George, had stuck the truncheon up his back passage. What she was also asked about, because one of the suggestions that is made to Mr Anqkar is that he knew that the defendant had received a substantial award of compensation for racial discrimination and that therefore, he knew that he got a lot of money. According to her, Mr Anqkar never told her anything about that. She also agreed that back in 2004 when they were living in Lancashire, which is where they appear to live now, Mr Anqkar was in debt and became bankrupt. He did transfer a property into her name, 'But I wasn't helping him in any way, he pleaded guilty to a bankruptcy offence.'

One of the problems of course, as I referred to in this

case, is the loss of documents. You will remember that Detective Sergeant Gadsby said well, the police records are now computerised. No document beyond the court records had been found in relation to the arrest of Mr Anqkar in 1986. They have been destroyed with the passage of time. There would have been a paper custody record but that was also destroyed. All other inquiries suggested that the papers had been destroyed and he made inquiries of the CPS as to whether they still had any papers for the court case and they would have been destroyed by now. You should therefore bear in mind what I told you about the direction of delay, that the loss or destruction of those documents may have the effect that lines of defence which might have been open to the defendant may have been closed off. Detective Sergeant Gadsby accepted the criticism that he should have made inquiries as to the exact age of Mr Anqkar at the time before deciding what charge to bring against the defendant. It was a mistake to charge him with the serious offence of indecent assault on somebody under the age of sixteen. He did confirm that nobody at Battersea recalls any officer having those ASPs at that time.

That is the prosecution case, you have the defendant's interview, I am not going to waste time or insult your intelligence by reading out to you a document you have in front of yourself. Take account of it, read it as a whole, do not extract individual answers out of context. So we go from there to the defendant's evidence.

Having chosen to give evidence, he does not have to

prove anything. It is not for him to prove he is innocent. What did he tell you? He told you about his police career. First of all, he dealt with his domestic circumstances. He has been married for thirty years; he has two grown-up children. He joined the Metropolitan Police in May 1982. He joined the crime squad at Battersea in 1985, served until 1989, dealing with a variety of offences attached sometimes to the murder squad, sometimes dealing with lesser things such as burglaries. Some undercover work dealing with street crime but mainly, he was in plain clothes. He produced a variety of documents confirming his progress through the police and obviously, he has a very respectable career in the police. Indeed, that was attested to by Mr Graham Markwick, former detective constable now retired who said how professional the defendant was. In due course, he would go on to move into other areas. Then, unfortunately, in 1998 he was investigated about an incident and there was a very poor investigation. He was accused of all sorts of things he had not done, distributing racist hate mail and at a very badly conducted disciplinary hearing he was dismissed but he fought the case to the employment tribunal and won the case. He was reinstated and received a large amount of compensation, and a full public apology. Thereafter, he resumed his police career, eventually, as I told you, reaching the rank of detective sergeant, with which rank he retired in May 2012.

As well mention them now. You have heard how Mr Markwick described the crime squad at Battersea, that it was well run, there was a good detective inspector running it and that the defendant was one of the well-respected members of this crime squad and he was a conscientious officer and, indeed, he recommended the defendant for various promotions because he regarded him as suitable for it. You will also remember that there was another feature of the case which may or may not be important. He was not at that stage an authorised police driver. That is one of the factors the defence rely upon because they say if he was not an authorised police driver, then there is no truth in what Mr Anqkar says about how the defendant was driving around in his police car, waving the truncheon at him as a way of intimidating or insulting him, because he was not a police driver at the time. The defence says that gives a lie to that suggestion.

If Mr Anqkar has made that up, you cannot rely on his evidence and if he has convinced himself that that is what happened, you cannot rely on his evidence there. You will remember there was another small detail as well about the tape-recorded interviews at the time of his arrest. At the time, they did not have tape recording but he said his solicitor at the time asked him for the tapes. Well, as I have said, you cannot deal with every single point but do bear in mind those points as you think they are important. Mr Virdi took you through the various documents showing his commendable career. You had character witnesses read, not only from fellow police officers but from other people.

Dr Richard Stone who worked on the inquiry into the

Stephen Lawrence murder, and that he spoke about the defendant's contribution. He made a submission to the inquiry and what Dr Stone said was that this confirmed some of the weaknesses in the investigation, and, indeed, that it led the inquiry to the conclusion we all know about, that at the time there was institutional racism in the Metropolitan Police. You had a statement read to you from Mr John McDonnell who is the MP for Hayes and Harlington, how he has known the defendant as an honest, responsible and caring person with a high degree of commitment to serving the community. Then you had a statement of Lord Singh of Wimbledon read to you. I cannot recall from his statement when he was elevated to the House of Lords but he is prominent as a seat representative within the inter-faith activities. He has met the defendant on a number of occasions and spoke about his good work in fighting racism in the Metropolitan Police and improving community relations. How his role in the Metropolitan Police Sikh Association and how he has been actively involved in his community? Indeed, perhaps more recently for the services rendered by Sikh and other Indian soldiers in the First World War. There are therefore all those character witnesses.

What did the defendant say about the actual event? He said, well, actually, he had no memory of arresting or detaining Mr Anqkar and he could not place him when he saw him in the witness box. That is perhaps not surprising because his appearance has probably altered quite a bit in the last twenty-nine years, as Mr Anqkar himself said.

He however explained to you how these documents work which existed at the time, the Arrest Form 74A and that if a case goes to court, there has to be a 74A, and one is missing. That is another of the difficulties which he faces. He, however, said positively: 'I didn't carry a truncheon on plain-clothes duties. I didn't have a collapsible truncheon, well, not until I was posted many years later to Ealing.' He confirmed, as Mr Makins did, that you do not carry much police equipment when you are doing that sort of work because you stand out.

'I have had experience of having to restrain people. Sometimes they do fight back or try to escape, not very often in the back of a police van but I totally deny (as he has always done throughout) using racist language towards Mr Anqkar. I totally deny assaulting in this way or committing any kind of indecent assault upon him.'

Well, he was cross examined about some of the allegations about the conspiracy which he thinks there is against him. You may think, members of the jury, that whether or not such a conspiracy exists or may exist is really what this case is all about. What this case is all about is whether you are sure that Mr Anqkar is a witness who is telling you the truth and somebody upon whom you can rely. Members of the jury, there is the evidence, let me just summarise the arguments.

The prosecution say that it can be established from such documentation as there is, the prosecution acknowledges that there is a lot of documentation missing, that the defendant was on duty at that time and he did deal with Mr Anqkar. The prosecution has to accept that Mr Makins does not provide supporting evidence for the indecent assault or for the possession of the truncheon. That there is, to some extent, variation between the two. You have to decide the consistency and inconsistency; you have to look at the chronology. In the end, the prosecution say well, Mr Makins is a significant witness. You can be sure that they were on duty and the defendant did what was alleged. The prosecution say you can be sure of all this on the evidence. What do the defence say? Well, when Mr Blaxland addressed you, he warned you of the dangers of taking, at face value, such accusations. He put it there is a real danger that events like the Jimmy Savile case provide a bandwagon for those with a grudge to jump on.

The defence say that you cannot be sure about the reliability or honesty of Mr Anqkar because of the discrepancies between his evidence and that of Mr Makins. There is also the fact that the documents are missing. Then you will remember what Mr Blaxland did yesterday was to focus on what he said were the ten lies which he says Mr Anqkar has told and that they give you very serious doubts as to whether you can rely upon his evidence at all. Among those lies was the one about the interview tape, about the use of the collapsible baton, the harassment by the defendant when he was not a police driver, his age, the Stanley knife, the injuries and so on. I have not gone through all of them, you will remember what Mr Blaxland said and you will take that all into account. In conclusion, what Mr Blaxland says to you when you look at the whole of the evidence in this case that whatever suspicions you may entertain about this at the highest, you cannot be sure that this defendant has acted in a way which will be wholly out of character as compared with what he has done throughout his police career.

Members of the jury, that is it, there is the evidence. There are the arguments. Which parts of the evidence and which arguments are important, that is for you to say and not me.

The jury retired to consider their verdict at 11:37 a.m.

HHJ: 'I will remain on the bench for a minute or two to let the jury get to their room. I do not want to meet them in the judge's corridor. Mr Blaxland, the defendant may have bail within the precincts of the court while the jury are considering their verdict. If the jury have not reached a verdict at the end of today, he may have bail over the weekend on exactly the same terms as have applied throughout the trial. I shall not take a verdict or deal with the jury question between 1 p.m. and 2 p.m. and the defendant is at liberty to leave court building between those hours.'
HB: 'Thank you very much.'

The jury returned into court at 12:37 p.m., after having reached a verdict.

CLERK: 'Will the defendant please stand. Will the foreman please stand. Mr foreman, please answer my first question with either a yes or a no. Has the jury reached verdicts upon which you are all agreed in relation to each count of the indictment?'

FOREMAN OF THE JURY: 'Yes.'

CLERK: 'On count one, charging the defendant with indecent assault of a male person, do you find the defendant guilty or not guilty?'

FOREMAN OF THE JURY: 'Not guilty.'

CLERK: 'You find the defendant not guilty, and is this your joint verdict?'

FOREMAN OF THE JURY: 'Yes.'

CLERK: 'In respect of count two, charging the defendant with misconduct in a public office, do you find the defendant guilty or not guilty?'

FOREMAN OF THE JURY: 'Not guilty.'

HHJ: 'Sit down.'

I had been found not guilty on both counts. A huge wave of relief washed over me and I suddenly felt rather emotional. Tears filled my eyes, but I quickly wiped them away as I wanted to remain calm and strong for the final few minutes in court.

CLERK: 'You find the defendant not guilty and that is your joint verdict.'

FOREMAN OF THE JURY: 'Yes.'

As the verdict was read and confirmed by the judge, a huge cheer came from the public gallery, which was very quickly stopped by the judge.

> HB: 'Ladies and gentlemen, please.'
> HHJ: 'I will not tolerate any disturbance in court … If people cannot control themselves they leave the court at once. That was a most unseemly outburst. It is not your fault, Mr Virdi, you may sit down. You are discharged, Mr Virdi. You may leave the dock in due course.'
> GV: 'Thank you, Your Honour.'

Judge Goymer then thanked the members of the jury for their important and invaluable role, and thanked both Evans and Henry.

> HHJ: 'Accordingly, with that, I thank you, members of the jury. I shall adjourn the court.'

CHAPTER 17

SCALES OF JUSTICE

As the court adjourned, I was finally released from the glass cage that I had spent the last week in. I rushed over to my family and friends, giving everybody a big hug. Sathat was particularly emotional and I could see the relief spread across her face.

As we left the court, I was met by Simon Israel, a reporter for *Channel 4 News*, who had been sitting alongside my family in the public gallery. I gave a short interview, which was later aired on the 7 p.m. news show. *Channel 4 News* presenter Jackie Long said:

An Asian former Met police sergeant, who won a series of race discrimination cases against the force, has been found not guilty of historical abuse. The judge in his summing up at Southwark Crown Court had said that a conspiracy against Gurpal Virdi may have been what this case was all about. Here is our home affairs correspondent, Simon Israel, who has been speaking exclusively to Gurpal Virdi.

The interview then cut to Simon:

In the words of the judge, Gurpal Virdi had a respected and distinguished career in the Met before retiring in 2012. Yet he found himself on trial this week, accused of racially and sexually abusing a sixteen-year-old in a police van back in 1986. The jury took less than an hour to clear him.

Images of me, Sathat and Matt coming out of court were then broadcast, before I gave my response to the ordeal: 'It is disturbing that the Metropolitan Police is still targeting me and my family year after year. This has to stop. People need to be held to account and sacked. This campaign, which has been ongoing since 1998, has to stop – it is not fair.'

The report cut back to Simon:

The Sikh officer came to prominence back in the '90s, when he was accused of sending racist hate mail to himself and other colleagues from ethnic backgrounds then trying to frame white officers for the crime. He was cleared by an employment tribunal and reinstated. A series of claims related to the racial discrimination he had faced resulted in nearly a quarter of a million pounds' pay-out by the Metropolitan Police. In retirement, he became the focus of another investigation, which lasted sixteen months, into allegations of historic abuse and the use of a collapsible baton.

The key question is how this case ever got to trial. The Met and the CPS got the age of the alleged victim wrong and as for the collapsible truncheon, well that was not available for at least another decade. A conspiracy against

Mr Virdi, said the judge today, may be what this case is all about.

'You say there is a conspiracy. Who do you say is behind the conspiracy?'

'There is a bit of conspiracy. There is incompetence as you have heard from the evidence – there is a lot of incompetence. Nothing was looked at properly. They saw my name and targeted me, yet again.'

'Why do you think they are targeting you?' asked Simon.

'Because I am the only person who is willing to stand up and fight against racism not only for police officers, but also for the community.'

Simon moved on to the Met-issued statement concerning my case.

The Metropolitan Police issued a statement tonight defending its investigation, saying: 'It would not have been proper to proceed in any other way. We presented the evidence to the Crown Prosecution Service who decided the allegations and evidence should be heard by a jury.'

The CPS, in turn, said there was sufficient evidence and serious issues were at stake. But for those who witnessed this trial, this case represents a worrying trend.

'From what I've heard, it feels very much like a witch hunt for an officer who has done something to a police force and they haven't liked it and they have made a decision to go down that path,' said National Black Police Association president Franstine Jones.

'Is that a proper way for a force to behave?' asked Simon.

'I don't think so, but it's not just something that happens in the Met, it happens in other forces up and down the country,' Franstine responded.

Simon continued with his report.

Mr Virdi has been a prominent figure in his area of west London. He was selected by Labour as a local councillor candidate but was suspended when he was charged just before the 2014 elections. He stood as an independent and won, and now his supporters want an inquiry into those who sanctioned this trial.

The report then concluded. What I have quoted isn't the report in its entirety; it was originally much longer as Simon and I also discussed the role of the IPCC.

After that we all went to the nearest pub, The Horniman at Hays, to celebrate. Although I was relieved that justice had been served, I couldn't help but think we were celebrating something that never should have gone to court in the first place.

CHAPTER 18

THE IPCC

After my interview with the police on 27 March 2014, I felt that I was being stitched up, so I contacted the Independent Police Complaints Commission (IPCC) to file a complaint against the Metropolitan Police. I received a standard, unhelpful letter asking me to direct my complaint to the police force concerned and they would then look into the matter. If I was unhappy with the outcome of my complaint, I would have the right to appeal to the IPCC. The letter also mentioned that 'the complaint will need to be sent to the DPS for consideration under the Police Reform Act'.

My complaint had been filed against the DPS, yet the IPCC were informing me that they – the same department that had made my life hell and subjected me to malicious allegations – would be looking into the matter. It was a bit like asking a thief to investigate a robbery they had committed. I objected, as I wanted an independent investigation, but the response I received from the IPCC was even worse:

Due to the contents of your complaint, the matter, as stated previously, has been raised internally. I appreciate your complaint is against the DPS therefore, upon receipt of your consent, we will pass the complaint to the head of the DPS, Commander Fiona Taylor. There is nothing further that the IPCC can do at this moment in time.

The IPCC's responses are scripted in order to control any complaints being made. The reason why I've chosen to include this chapter is to show that the IPCC is not a truly independent body – the police will still investigate complaints made about the force. Although officially independent from the police, many of the IPCC investigators are former or current officers, and therefore cannot remain impartial. The Home Secretary funds the IPCC and appoints its commissioners, but the organisation is allegedly free from government interference.

There is a total lack of confidence in the system, so it is no wonder that many people choose not to register their complaints. Having worked as an officer and having spoken to people from various backgrounds, particularly those from BAME communities in London, I knew that complainants were not getting the independent support that they needed and officers were not being held to account. The IPCC is now generally seen as a body that acts only to whitewash police wrongdoing – especially in cases involving deaths in police custody. I was now their victim.

Many people now choose to pursue the police force via the courts rather than through the IPCC, whose main course of action will be to gather all of the evidence a complainant had provided and pass this to the police. But the problem is that a complainant will have limited funds to fight a legal battle, whereas the police do not have the same financial constraints and can put their money behind their officers. This often results in some complainants choosing to drop their cases.

The IPCC has failed to deal with many allegations of police racism and assault, deaths in custody, corruption and unlawful arrests. Even when there is overwhelming evidence, the officer concerned is often allowed to retire or the matter will be dealt with internally by the force involved and ultimately dropped.

I gave up because I knew that my complaint would not be investigated impartially.

The IPCC needs to be disbanded.

CHAPTER 19

THE WHITEWASH CONTINUES

It was Thursday 3 March 2016. I hadn't been feeling well – my energy levels had dropped and I found myself often fatigued – so I had arranged to see my GP that morning. He wrote me a prescription of iron tablets and gave me vitamin B12 injections. That evening I had a council meeting, so I thought I would head into the town centre early and pop into the bank. On my way there, I passed by the police station. I decided to go in. Dressed in a suit, I immediately caught the attention of the station officer, who came over and asked if there was anything he could help me with.

'I'm here to report a crime,' I said.

'OK, I'll get someone to see you immediately,' replied the officer on duty. I noted from his shoulder number that he was a special constable. I sat down; there were other people in the room and they were staring right at me. Within about five minutes, I was called to a private counter where PC Syed dealt with me. Once he knew who I was and that I wanted to report a case of perjury (making false statements and per- verting the course of justice), he immediately went to speak to his supervising officer. He returned and started filling out a CRIS report.

While this was happening, other officers had realised who I was and came over to greet me. The special constable who I had spoken with told me that he had been a police driver during the '80s and PC Syed told me that he had just been appointed a neighbourhood officer in Cranford.

I explained about my case and said Anqkar had to be investigated for perjury. Once the report was logged, I was given a crime reference number: 3006371/16. Having reported the crime, I left the police station to attend my meeting at the civic centre.

Unsurprisingly, I did not hear back from Hounslow police: not even a letter or an email to acknowledge that I had made a complaint. It wasn't until more than five months later, on 16 August 2016, that I received an email out of the blue from a Mark Lake, a lawyer who was writing to me on behalf of the Police Federation. His email stated:

> I was also contacted today by DC John Hughes of Walworth CID, who is investigating the allegation of perjury against Anqkar. He had been dumped with volumes of paper including the trial transcript and wanted my 'insight' for want of better word because he needed a starting point before making his way through the mass of paper.
>
> I sent him my letter of claim wherein we identified fifteen strands of lack of honesty on the part of Anqkar. In order to avert any suggestion of bias or lack of objectivity,

I also sent a copy of the response so that he had a balanced view and could reach his own conclusions.

Obviously he is not part of the DPS, and on the face of it is impartial. From the tone of our conversation, he sounded like a decent bloke and no stooge. You may or may not have any faith in the process.

I have only one question at this stage. If he wants to speak to you, would you assist him?

I agreed to speak to him, although I knew it would be a waste of time because the Met always protects its own officers – which is probably why it had been almost six months before anyone contacted me. No doubt there were meetings held amongst senior members of staff on how best to deal with this.

Detective Inspector John Hughes from Southwark CID informed me that he would be investigating the allegations that I'd made against Anqkar. He assured me that he was totally independent from the DPS and that he would do his utmost to get to the bottom of the case. I remember thinking at the time that it was the usual crap that officers feed you in order to win you over, so that they can find out what evidence you have and use it to write off the crime report that you've filed.

On 29 September 2016, I received the following letter:

Dear Mr Virdi,

As you know I have been asked to assess the legitimacy

of your perjury allegation (Crime report – 3006371/16). To that end I have reviewed the following documents provided to me:

1. Note of proceedings, relating to your trial starting on 17 July 2015
2. Summing-Up to verdict by HHJ Goymer
3. Letter from your solicitor, Cartwright King, to the Directorate of Legal Services dated 10 February 2016
4. Reply from Mr Andrew Fairbrother of Directorate of Legal Services dated 20 May 2016

Section 1 of the Perjury Act 1911 creates the offence of wilfully giving false evidence:

s.1(1) If any person lawfully sworn as a witness or as an interpreter in a judicial proceeding wilfully makes a statement material in that proceeding, which he knows to be false or does not believe to be true, he shall be guilty of perjury.

You allege that Wasim Anqkar lied during your trial relating to an allegation of sexual assault and malfeasance in a public office. The incident in question took place in October 1986. At the conclusion of proceedings, you were acquitted on both counts.

I have decided not to progress the investigation as I believe it would not be proportionate to do so for the following reasons:

The area that you identify as lies by Mr Anqkar during

the trial, which are comprehensively covered in the Cart-wright King letter, strike me as inconsistencies that Mr Blaxland QC identified and expertly asserted in your favour to the court.

HHJ Goymer eloquently explains the difficulties that historical investigations face in the section he refers to as 'Delay'. This delay direction makes it clear that 'the memory can play tricks' and what witnesses 'believe to be their clear recollection is totally distorted and inaccu-rate'. His Honour then goes on to explain that delay has deprived you of putting forward a positive defence due to witnesses being untraceable and court documents being lost or destroyed through the passage of time. Therefore, I am satisfied that an investigation into your allegation of perjury would not produce any further evidence regarding the circumstances of the October 1986 incident that could be used in an investigation into Mr Anqkar. All reasona-ble lines of inquiry have already been conducted by the Directorate of Professional Standards and subsequently assessed by the CPS.

With regard to the wilful element of the offence, I have to consider if Mr Anqkar provided the lies that you iden-tify deliberately or intentionally, rather than accidentally or mistakenly. Again, I believe that HHJ Goymer's delay direction more than takes account of this issue: 'People can have a fixed idea in their own minds about how events were and that may be completely different to reality.'

For the reasons above, I cannot in good faith authorise

an investigation funded from the public purse and the crime report will now be closed.

Yours sincerely,

John Hughes

Detective Inspector

I showed the letter to Sathat, whose response was: 'What were you expecting? Some justice to be done? You knew that was never going to happen.'

'I know, but I had to go down this route before I could close it,' I said. 'It just shows how corrupt the system is – you can't go to the police, the IPCC, or any government department to expose this type of behaviour. No wonder people lose hope.'

Sathat was scathing: 'The first line says it all, "I have been asked to assess the legitimacy of your perjury allegations"; they don't even believe you. I'm sure that when victims go to the police to make allegations of a crime that police officers don't assess the legitimacy of the allegations first.'

I agreed with Sathat: 'You're right, crimes are reported and investigated. Anqkar lied in that witness box and everyone in court knew that. That's why they didn't provide John Hughes with the full transcript of the hearing. DI Hughes didn't investigate my allegation that false statements were given, as he was too concerned with Anqkar. Furthermore, all of his information was given to him by the Directorate of Legal Services – no doubt they probably wrote the letter for him as well.

Their problem is that if Anqkar is charged and put in front of a court, he's not going to go down quietly, he's going to spill the beans on the officers who encouraged and coached him – that's why the Met are concerned.'

Given that so many senior officers and the CPS were involved in my case – and the numerous gaps and mistakes in the prosecution's evidence, as outlined by my defence team and MPs such as Sir Peter Bottomley – there is clear evidence that police corruption and cover-ups continue to this day. There have been numerous inquiries and reports into police practices over the years – Lord Scarman's report after the 1981 Brixton riots, and the inquiry into the 1993 murder of Stephen Lawrence. Every time, these official reports conclude that vital lessons must be learnt. However, as my case and subsequent fight for justice clearly illustrate, this has not yet happened. The whitewash continues.

As the reader will be aware, I have taken steps to anonymise the complainant in the case, as he is legally entitled to anonymity for life despite the jury finding me not guilty of the allegations he made against me. As this book was being prepared for press, I was reminded by Southwark Crown Court that breaching the complainant's right to anonymity would be a contempt of court. The reader can draw their own conclusions about the justice of law that protects those who make false allegations and silences the innocent.

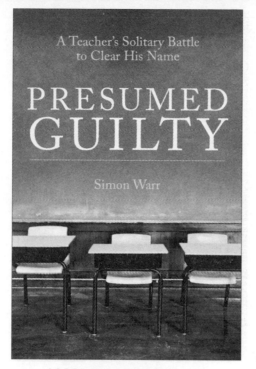

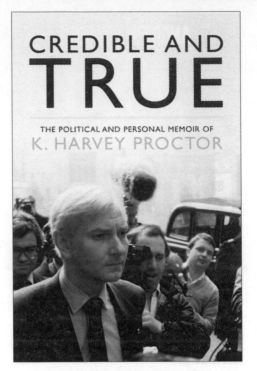

496PP HARDBACK, £20

Early in the morning of 4 March 2015, a fierce knock at the door heralded the start of a new chapter in Harvey Proctor's almost continuous relationship with the police and media, when officers from the Metropolitan Police raided his home in connection with Operation Midland, Scotland Yard's investigation into allegations of a historical Westminster paedophile ring.

In *Credible and True* – words famously used by the police to describe the allegations of Proctor's traducer – the former Conservative MP talks frankly about his life in and out of Parliament, from the struggles and controversy surrounding his resignation in 1987 to the numerous homophobic attacks endured since – one of which, revealed here in horrific detail for the first time, was a very nearly successful attempt on his life.

Finally, he speaks candidly about his most recent embroilment in Operation Midland, of being the victim of a 'homosexual witch-hunt' that has all but destroyed his reputation, adding to the topical debate about police lack of due process in the post-Savile world of 'guilty until proven innocent'.